MW00935973

Sand Dollars & Swiss Cheese

FACING RARE DISEASE WITH AN EVER-FAITHFUL GOD

Amber McCall

WESTBOW
PRESS®
A DIVISION OF THOMAS NELSON
& ZONDERVAN

This book is a work of non-fiction. Unless otherwise noted, the author and the publisher make no explicit guarantees as to the accuracy of the information contained in this book and in some cases, names of people and places have been altered to protect their privacy.

WestBow Press books may be ordered through booksellers or by contacting:

WestBow Press
A Division of Thomas Nelson & Zondervan
1663 Liberty Drive
Bloomington, IN 47403
www.westbowpress.com
844-714-3454

ISBN: 978-1-6642-7663-5 (sc)
ISBN: 978-1-6642-7664-2 (hc)
ISBN: 978-1-6642-7662-8 (e)

Library of Congress Control Number: 2022915959

Print information available on the last page.

WestBow Press rev. date: 01/12/2023

CONTENTS

DEDICATION PAGE

This book is dedicated to my favorite person, Chris.

PREFACE

God asked me to document my story. I was afraid. Afraid of what people would think of me or that they might treat me differently once they read about my life. He quickly reminded me that it's not my story, but His story that He is telling through me. I needed that reminder. The reminder that I'm not responsible for this–God is. He is in control, and the only reason I continue with this smile and positive outlook is because I have the God of the universe on my side. A God who has proven time and again that He conquers death, that He deserves the glory, and that He has the power and ability to give and take away.

All of these stories are 99.2% factual–I have changed many of the names of those involved in order to protect their identity, although I am forever grateful for the ways in which they have impacted the course of my life and forged me into the person I am today. For what are we without the people we associate with? Lonely souls, that's what.

ACKNOWLEDGMENT

I am thankful first and foremost for the Lord. Of course, this story would sound very different if it weren't for His faithfulness and goodness. Secondly, I'm forever grateful for my husband who has been a constant support through all things. Thirdly, I extend a large 'thank you' to Ms. Betsey Newenhuyse, my editor, who prayed with me for the impact of this book and encouraged me as a writer. I also want to acknowledge and thank Pastor Mark Tobey who saw potential in this work in its infancy and my Sunday Night Bible Study ladies for their consistent prayers and cheerleading.

Rightly, I cannot forget to thank my mother and sister who have also defended this message from the beginning.

Last but not least, I am grateful for Dr. K, Ms. Barb Roches, Ms. Melissa Castorena, and Ms. Hannah Tobey for their willingness to read the early drafts and share their knowledge and unique perspectives with me.

INTRODUCTION

To the one still fighting for a diagnosis, keep telling your story.
To the one struggling through each day, seek the little moments of joy.
To the one feeling lost and lonely, you are not alone.
To the one caring for a loved one dealing with a terrible disease, you are so valuable.
To the one reading to learn more about the life of another, thank you for your courage and curiosity.
To the one facing a situation that feels out of your control, persevere.

Rare disease is not rare. Over 300 million people in the world suffer from one of the over 7,000 rare diseases that sneak their way into our lives and cause us to question all we knew before the twinge of back pain, swelling in our arm, or daily headaches. The list of symptoms is endless, as are the hours spent in waiting rooms and hospital beds, but the strength, courage, and resilience that has been shining in you through it all is starting to speak to the world. Find a way to let it.

It is my hope and prayer that, as you read this story, you would feel that strength empower you, that courage push you forward, and that resilience spring you into action. God is writing a story with your life, and you have the choice to keep it to yourself or to share it with the world so that people may see His good works and He would receive the glory. Our God cares deeply for you and will continue to provide endlessly for you as you trust Him with your story.

Living with a rare disease (or three) is not an easy feat, but it is an opportunity to show the world how much of a fighter you are. It is an opportunity to push on with a sense of adventure and a spirit of hope that will gracefully (and sometimes not so much) lead you to the finish line. I look forward to the day when I get to hear about the mountains you moved, the symptoms you crushed, the people you changed, and those who changed you. Keep fighting, warrior!

1

"We're just not sure."

"Three ... two ... one ... Happy New Year!" It wasn't an ideal place to ring in 1999. As everyone around me celebrated, I sat in my hospital bed and wondered where the nurse had put the pan because my tummy just wouldn't stop its gymnastics routine. In fact, it'd been trying to go for the gold since early that morning. Like so many times before, the doctors just weren't sure what was wrong with me. *This time* they ruled out the possibility of meningitis, but only because I could touch my chin to my chest, despite the fact that I couldn't keep anything down and had a migraine larger than life. Little did I know, the "we're just not sure" diagnosis would be the number one hit for the next twenty years of my life.

We'll get to that. First, a little background building (I'm a bilingual teacher; that's what I do). My navy parents met in the bar from the movie Top Gun, got married, and shortly after, had me— born at the naval hospital on the base in San Diego, California, in the spring of 1988. I would love to say we stayed there, and I grew up on the beach—well, I did, but not that one. Our family of three was transferred to San Antonio, Texas, when I was about eight months old. We stayed for less than a year and then found ourselves on another beach in Charleston, South Carolina.

In Charleston, we were greeted with strong winds and torrential rain as Hurricane Hugo hit the shores in September 1989. I don't have memories of the storm, but I have seen footage (recorded on a large camcorder with an actual VHS tape—if you don't know what that is, google it!) of me with beautiful tan baby rolls wearing nothing but a diaper, eating an apple larger than my head, and walking around outside during the eye of the hurricane. Actually to be fair, I don't think I was allowed outside, but I have seen the video evidence of the huge trees that fell and the cars that were flipped over in our neighborhood. Our country has seen plenty of devastation caused by horrible hurricanes in the past few years, but I hear Hugo was a monster of a storm as well! Thankfully, our family stayed safe by hiding in our bathtub under a mattress. It sounds like a joke, but it's not.

My brother endured the storm in utero and was born late that fall. I quickly had someone to translate for! I was the best big sister and made sure he got all of his needs met, especially when that meant we both got what we wanted. As I mentioned, we grew up on the beach, eating sand and building sand castles. You know, the drip ones where you hold wet sand in the air until it spills onto itself and starts to resemble a stalagmite. Those were my favorite!

Sand dollars make up the other part of my Charleston memories. I remember the adults would wade far out into the ocean (Okay, only about twenty yards or so, but for a three-year-old that's far!) and rake their toes through the sand. Eventually, someone would dive head-first into the water and after what seemed like an eternity, pull out a gross-looking green disc. Waiting for the disc to dry in the sun for a few hours was the hard part, and what was worse, after all that wait, we could finally clean off all the algae and seaweed only to wait some more! Several days later, the coolest thing would happen. My mom or dad would break the sand dollar in half and tiny pieces would come out. We called them angel wings.

Okay, we've waited so long for the angel wings that it's now the spring of 1992 (I told you it seemed like a really, *really* long time), during which my baby sister was born. By this point, I was a four-year-old, walking, talking machine telling the world about how cool my little brother was and how I was going to take the best care of my little sister. My mom had left the navy at this point, but my dad was finishing nursing school, so he had to stay in Charleston. Since I was about to start school, my mom moved the three of us kids to her parents' house in Green Bay, Wisconsin, our third move. I attended Pilgrim Lutheran for 4K and don't remember much of it other than the fact that I did not like milk patrol because it meant I had to carry that ugly plastic bin into the dark, scary basement with an uncooperative boy.

Like many girls who grew up in the nineties, I was adorned with larger-than-life scrunchies and hair bows, stirrup leggings (you know, the ones with the elastic under your feet so they didn't ride up—if you're younger than me, these might be as foreign as the VCR and camcorder), and some sort of awful, colorful windbreaker or mock turtleneck. I do remember one birthday when I was gifted a *super cool* purple Beauty and the Beast skirt that had roses all over it. Disney movies were "totally tubular" and so were the TMNT (Teenage Mutant Ninja Turtles for those of you who don't know). I spent my days playing teacher in our vintage school desks (those would be so "in" right now) or playing mom to my Baby Alive doll. I also grew to love Polly Pockets and Pound Puppies. Man, Pokémon Go has nothing on those Pound Puppies which quickly became bartering tools in my elementary school. They were adorable, tradeable, and pretty easily hideable. Now that I am a teacher, I know how annoyed our teachers were by them; I was clueless about that then. I still remember being in the corner of the dark basement (why didn't my schools turn the lights on?) negotiating with my prized possessions like they meant the world.

That dark basement was at one of the most important schools I've attended (although all of them were pretty important). When I was five, my mom made the decision to enroll my siblings and me in a Catholic school called St. Thomas Moore, or STM. This school played a huge role in defining who I am today because it was there that I became a Christian. Now, I don't have a Saul-turned-Paul moment (Acts 9:1–19) in my faith, and although I struggled with that for a while, I've come to terms with it. That being said, those years I spent at STM were formative in my walk with the Lord. I learned stories from the Bible and learned that Jesus Christ died on the cross for my sins and the sins of the world. It's where I wrestled with the fact that God is three persons in one (God the Father, Jesus the Son, and the Holy Spirit). Those big truths quickly made their way into my heart. I am so thankful for my parents' decision to choose two Christian schools early in my education. I am also thankful for my mom's continued support of those truths in my everyday life.

Every morning before school, we would recite Psalm 118:24, and my mom would pray for a hedge of protection around us. She spoke truth into our lives, she wrote it out on index cards and hung them around the house, and she had us write out scripture as well. The purpose of doing all that was to instill the Word in our lives, and because of her diligence, God's words influence my life consistently and faithfully. We have all had that moment when we realize that the things our parents made us do as children, which we often dreaded, have become the very things of most importance. As an adult, I cherish those memories and am grateful that my mom instilled a love of God's Word into my life. God speaks through His Word.

STM was life-changing in another way as well. It was where I developed what became a lifelong love of learning. I was a self-motivated, goal-oriented student, which helped in many situations throughout my life. We'll get to those. Anyway, as I implied, I loved school! The weekly spelling tests were my jam, and when it came to the annual spelling bee my stomach was in knots from both excitement and nerves. You see, in first and second grade, I competed pretty publicly with the smartest boy in the class, an

"Albert Einstein." I remember having several philosophical debates with him over things like from what height someone could safely jump on the playground or what the statistical likelihood was that we would have tacos again at lunch. It was near the end of second grade when Albert and I finally had a chance to go head-to-head when it mattered most–the spelling bee. We suffered through something like eighteen rounds before it was down to the two of us. It was his turn, and Mrs. Moore handed him the word on a silver platter. To my delight, however, he spelled it incorrectly, and it was all I could do not to hula dance as I correctly spelled the word *lei* and became the spelling bee champ! The coolest thing about it? We were in a combined second and third grade, so I was the champ of two grades.

Although my elementary school years were filled with laughter, gym scooters, Lisa Frank folders, and BFF sleepovers, I remember spending an innumerable amount of mornings and afternoons in the nurse's office with migraines. Now, I'm not sure that many people would believe an eight-year-old having to go to the nurse several times a week for migraines, but that high-achieving-student side of me gave me some credibility. As an elementary school teacher now, if a student even asks me to go to the nurse before he or she has thrown up, I somewhat roll my eyes (I'm not heartless, just realistic), but there are a few students who you know are telling the truth. I was telling the truth, and the adults in my life were starting to worry a bit.

My parents decided to bring me to the doctor to see what he could see. Surprisingly, he didn't see very much. I had my eyes tested to no avail (I had perfect vision). They checked my diet, my physical fitness, and even did an MRI. Remember earlier when I mentioned "we're just not sure"? Yes, I heard it a lot as a child. No one could explain the chronic headaches. Even stranger than the headaches, no one could explain why one of my eyes appeared larger than the other.

Was I losing my mind? How come these medical professionals couldn't figure out what was wrong with me? I knew that daily migraines were not normal, nor was the knee pain, but I was starting to doubt that I would ever get proper answers. Despite the frustration and hopelessness, I would continue to seek help. It wasn't an easy path, nor a short one. I continued getting weird stares and questioning glances from many doctors which had me often questioning my sanity. Thankfully, even if I faced some criticism along the way, it wouldn't always be like that.

> Continue to share your symptoms and pain with doctors, despite their misunderstandings and unbelief. You will eventually find someone who can confirm what you've been saying all along.

The fact that my eyes are different sizes has always really bothered me. I think it stemmed from when I changed schools between fourth and fifth grade. I remember not really liking the idea of being the new kid on the block (it wasn't as cool as that music group NKOTB made it seem). It didn't help that one of the boys I played soccer with at recess, we will call him Lionel Messi, decided that it was weird that my eyes were different sizes and that I had huge teeth (oh yeah, like really big–once compared to chiclets by a mean girl in high school). Anyway, he had an endearing nickname for me that all the other children decided to use as well: Igor. Flattering, I know. Especially as a young girl new to a school and trying to fit in. We've all been there—fitting in is not easy—being called Igor doesn't make it any easier. Little did I know, Lionel and I would have many encounters over the years and would later become friends. Luckily, I got the votes later in high school to beat him for a seat as Junior Class President. I can't remember if he ever apologized for creating that awful nickname, but I'm pretty sure when I brought it up to him several years later, he didn't even remember. (Lionel, if you're reading this, I forgave you a long time ago).

but I say,
love
your enemies!
pray
for those
who persecute
you!

Matthew
5:44
NLT

Forgiveness is important.

Jesus calls us to love our enemies in Matthew 5:44. He emphasizes the importance of forgiveness later in Matthew 18 by telling us that we should forgive our brother seventy-seven times. Wow! That's a lot of forgiveness. Sometimes, the things other people do to us hurt, but it's important that we extend grace to them just as Jesus did for us. Think about it. He suffered inhumanely and died on a cross for the forgiveness of OUR sins: you, me, your neighbor, your friends. We are all forgiven for every bad thing we've ever done as long as we accept that Jesus saved us on that cross. What a sacrifice.

Moment for Reflection

1. What is the most difficult thing you've ever had to forgive?

2. As hard as forgiveness is, what are the benefits for the one doing the forgiving?

2

Night Games &
the Three B's

It was New Year's Eve. Yes, the one from the beginning of this book. You saw how miserable I was lying in that bed. I was ten, and I wanted to be eating too much candy and playing UNO as I watched the ball drop in Times Square to welcome in 1999. Instead, I was pumped with antibiotics as I listened to my parents convince the doctors not to do a lumbar puncture. The truth of the matter was that I was very sick, but no one knew why. Looking back, I am almost positive that I had aseptic meningitis (swelling of the meninges caused by something other than a bacterial infection), but I was not diagnosed at the time.

Thankfully, as a resilient ten-year-old, I quickly recovered and was back to my old self, becoming friends with Ramona Quimby and Anne of Green Gables when I wasn't playing "night games" like kick the can with my real-life friends. When I think back on the time we spent playing outside, and remember the stories of my dad and his friends galavanting through the neighborhoods on their bikes at all hours of the night (okay, maybe not ALL hours), my heart breaks a bit for the children of today who spend so much time with their faces in front of screens. Don't get me wrong, technology is amazing in some regards (so thankful for my car's remote start in the winter!), but nothing beats playing outside, hanging out face to face with other wonderful humans, and experiencing nature.

> Pursue a "normal" childhood for your kiddos at all costs—despite your fears and/or anxieties as a parent. Let them explore in the park, eat sand, discover insects and animals, and learn about sharing and teamwork with other kiddos.

Speaking of nature, several of my most favorite childhood memories involve the great outdoors. We took several family road trips out west to see our cousins in Arizona. It was such an exciting thing—even planning and packing for the trip was amazing. I remember my mom having to call (on a landline) national parks and hotels for brochures that we would then receive in the mail and spend hours looking at (so thankful for the internet for when I plan our road trips these days!). Once we decided where we wanted to go, my parents planned our route and my mom would print out maps and make each of us a guidebook that we used on the trip. It was required that we highlight our route on the map and even keep track of gas prices at each stop. Yes, as an overachiever, I documented the amount of gas we purchased, calculated the total price, and sometimes even figured out how many miles to the gallon we were getting in our old blue Ford Windstar (#nerdalert).

The memories we have from those trips are priceless, and I could probably write a book just on those, so I won't share them all, but I do want to share a few things with you. The first is a story that I'll call "The Three B's." It had been very dry that summer, and we were somewhere in either Wyoming or Montana where they close down campgrounds when there is a chance of fire. Due to the dryness, there were a lot of closed sites, and dusk was creeping in. The next site we drove to was open! As we drove in, my brother pointed out that he didn't see any other tents in the campground. Despite that observation, my dad pulled into site #4 and the three of us jumped out of the van. My mom stepped out after we had begun to throw around the frisbee, and she quickly called us over. She was pointing to something on the ground and saying that we couldn't stay here.

"But mooooooommmmm, every other campground was closed." I complained as I made my way over to see what the big deal was. To my surprise, I suddenly found myself in agreement with her "let's high-tail it out of here" attitude as I recognized the prints on the ground as bear paws (the first B). No way was I about to share my sleeping bag or even my breakfast with a bear!

We packed back into the van and drove a couple more miles down the road. The sun was about to set when another open campground came into view. Finding a campsite wasn't hard because there was only one other car in the whole place. My dad parked, and we all worked together to pitch the tent as fast as we could, since we were already doing it by lantern light. I'm sure a few games of Kings Corners were played before we brushed our teeth in the bushes and then went to sleep.

The next morning, I awoke to the delicious smell of bacon (the second B). I don't think I'm alone in the belief that bacon is amazing. So, as most of you would probably do, I threw on a sweatshirt and headed toward the door of the tent. As I unzipped it, I stopped dead in my tracks as I stared at a giant bobcat (you guessed it, the third B) twenty feet in front of me. Thankfully, there was about a ten-foot creek between me and that bobcat, but remember when I said there was bacon? That bobcat must've been a fan like the rest of us because he was doing his best to find a way over to our side of the creek. I remember him pacing along the banks of the river. Once my parents realized it, we took down the tent and fit everything back in the vehicle in record time. I locked my door as I said a prayer of thanksgiving that I didn't get eaten by a bobcat. To my dismay though, I never did get any bacon–so that's a pretty bittersweet ending, wouldn't ya say?

That bobcat wasn't the only wild animal we saw on our trips out west. My family had close encounters with moose, buffalo, elk, mule deer, road runners (yes, they are real), prairie dogs, and so many other cool looking animals that we don't usually see in the midwest. One of the reasons I loved Yellowstone was because of all of the wildlife. I mean, every half mile you would see a car or two pulled off to the side of the road and people standing in the grass pointing into the gulch or up the mountain at a pack of wolves or herd of buffalo (that were not always at a safe distance).

If you have never been in the American West, I encourage you to get yourself there. Some of the most spectacular sunsets, majestic mountains, and beautiful landscapes I have seen have been on those trips. When you make it out there, make sure to spend some time at Mesa Verde and the Badlands (my favorites). Of course, there is The Grand Canyon which speaks for itself, but is truly a sight to behold in person (although it is also amazing in photographs). On top of that (no pun intended), there are the Rocky Mountains. Words almost can't describe these monsters (it's a wonder no one's ever written a song about them—). We had some treacherous drives on those mountain roads, saw a few goats, sat in "traffic" when they were blasting out a new bridge with dynamite, and were literally above the clouds, which is simultaneously one of the coolest and scariest experiences one can have. The list continues with Mount Rushmore, the natural hot springs (where we had a "wow, we live in such a small world" moment when we met two other Wisconsin families in a hot spring in Wyoming), The Redwood Forest (someone should really throw those in a song somewhere too while they're at it), and Disneyland–if you're into that kind of thing (SBB, if you're reading this, I love you).

Another really quick animal story. On our way to Crater Lake, we had driven up the California coast into Oregon and stopped on the beach. Strolling along, I noticed some clear goo on the sand and bent down to investigate. My brother prodded it with a stick (I want to say gently, but I'd probably be lying), as my dad informed us it was a dead jellyfish. On that same beach, we also found two starfish that, if I remember correctly, my sister begged my dad to keep as passengers on our adventure in the van (I wonder what happened to those guys). After all that excitement, we continued on our way to Crater Lake. With its grandeur and beauty it kept up the excitement. It is a sunken volcano (Mount Mazama) in the middle of a beautiful, deep, blue, mountain lake.

I hope you have a few new places to google now, but I must get on with the rest of the story. I'm still only in middle school at this point! When I wasn't on a trip during the summer, I was playing softball. I had been playing since I was eight and had fallen in love with the smell, the energy, and the teamwork. I played on the All-star team all three years of middle school and had such a good time with my teammates and my coaches. We had a coach, I'll call him Gilbert, who made the game even more exciting with his anecdotes, encouragement, and willingness to be silly with us. I am grateful for his ability to push us to achieve while allowing us to enjoy the game. We won several tournaments over the years thanks to his leadership, and while playing for him, I learned a lot about the kind of leader I wanted to be when I grew up.

Cross-country trips and softball tournaments weren't all fun and games though. I remember having to often make the conscious decision to bench myself. Dealing with debilitating symptoms of easily-incurred dehydration, I watched on as my siblings and friends lived a normal, uninhibited life. My parents were constantly reminding me to drink water out of sixty-four-ounce Big Gulps cups in Arizona to ensure my swimming days didn't get cut short. Despite my valiant water-drinking efforts (do they have an Olympic sport for that?), for some reason, the headaches and lethargy didn't seem to plague me as much in the air conditioning, so that's usually where I felt the best physically.

Listen to your body. Even if it's difficult to sit on the sidelines, rest when you need to.

As I floated awkwardly through middle school as the best of us do, school came easily to me and I often found myself bored in class. This gave me an opportunity to help my peers, which is probably the first time I realized I might like to be a teacher someday. Although I enjoyed showing others how to use the Pythagorean theorem and editing papers for people, I dreamt of becoming a lawyer and fighting to defend people's rights. What an awesome way to help your fellow human beings.

Embracing the awkwardness (although we definitely didn't always realize how awkward we were), my friends and I always attended school dances and swayed back and forth to "With Arms Wide Open" and other classics of the time. Sporting events and open gyms were frequented by my group of friends, and I remember that getting out of school early to get ready for a game or travel to another school for a match was so exciting! On this occasion, we got out of the eighth period early for a home volleyball match when I was in seventh grade. Everyone we knew was there, including my eighth grade crush. My team played second, and since my friend forgot her shoes, I let her borrow mine. Note: this meant I was not wearing shoes and in fact only had socks on.

My friend, Jasmine, was a strong-armed server and practically won the match for us! Exhilarated by her amazing performance (which was probably in part to the wearing of my shoes), I bounded down the bleachers until I lost my footing and proceeded to roll head over heels down the last four or five before hitting my head on the gym floor. Talk about embarrassing! That alone would have been enough to send me into hibernation, but all of that happened right in front of that cute boy I had a crush on. Yikes, I was never going to show my face at school again! I headed into the locker room with some of my teammates laughing by my side until they realized I was bleeding and had a raging headache. Needless to say, my pleas to transfer schools were snuffed out by my parents, and I showed up the next day with a plump lip and a deflated pride balloon, but I survived. At the time, I had no idea how serious of an injury that fall could have caused.

My eighth grade year brought some highs and some lows. I was at the top of my class, running for student council class president, and thankful to finally be in some advanced classes. Things were going pretty well, but remember Lionel from earlier? Yeah, I lost the election to him because he bribed everyone with candy. Oh well, I had other things to worry about, like when my world came crumbling down around me and my siblings when my dad told us that he and my mom were getting a divorce. I was devastated. Absolutely blindsided. Sure, they had had arguments, and our life wasn't perfect, but from the inside, it was seemingly pretty awesome. My parents were both very involved in our lives, from academics to sports, and as I mentioned before, we enjoyed our family vacations. I couldn't believe my ears as he sat the three of us down and explained that he would be moving out.

Thankfully, my mom anticipated the difficult days ahead and contacted a teacher for each of us. Those loving souls watched out for us at school, checked in to make sure we were surviving, and continued to be a safe space to cry or laugh in while at school. The teacher my mom called for me was Mrs. Graphing. She was one of those teachers you never forget. You know the one: funny, kind, amazing at explaining things like algebra, but also someone you can talk to and trust. Mrs. Graphing was all of those things, and I was so grateful for her kindness that Monday, when I went to school after my dad's "news." She approached me that morning and offered some sweet words and then gave me a gift to cheer me up. I don't remember everything that was in the bag, but the little wind-up walking heart still brings a smile to my face when I think about it. That was the second time that I considered the teaching profession–to be able to bring joy to a child in the midst of heartache–what an honor!

As the oldest, I didn't have much of a chance to grieve my old life (everything I had known up to this point seemed to have become obsolete pretty quickly) as I needed to be a symbol of strength for my siblings. The devastation hit me hard in the beginning, but I made my peace with it (or at least I thought I did) and then tried to console my brother and sister. My brother was in sixth grade and my sister was in fourth grade. Divorce is never easy, but we were all old enough to be used to the life we were living, to be thrown off when it changed, and to remember the experience and feel its effects. Having to travel between houses during the week was a bummer (thankfully, my dad only moved less than a mile away), and facing the questions from friends was not easy. My siblings and I have never really discussed how the divorce impacted each one of us, but I am grateful I was old enough to realize that what was going on between my parents wasn't my fault. I'm not so sure my siblings realized this important truth.

My heart broke for my mom, as I watched her put her feelings aside (at least in front of us) and continue to pour her heart and soul into raising us the best she could. We didn't have extravagant things, but we always had food on the table and clothes on our backs. DIY was the name of the game, which I have continued to play into adulthood. Keep in mind that this was all pre-Pinterest—I'm sure many of her projects would have been re-pinned endlessly. She was cutting old jeans and sewing diaper bags out of them and wrapping gifts with twine and red wooden beads. Way ahead of her time!

She also made sure that we were able to participate in the activities that we loved, even if it meant she worked extra hours that month. Now that I am older, I know how much she sacrificed to make a good life for us, despite the chasm of heartache in her own life. For that, I am forever grateful. I admire her independence, perseverance, and willingness to do what was necessary in the face of adversity.

Instead be kind to each other, tenderhearted, forgiving one another, just as God through Christ has forgiven you.

Ephesians 4:32
NLT

Forgiveness is *still* important.

At the end of chapter 1, I discussed what the Bible has to say about forgiveness and why it is so important. At the time, I wanted to believe I had forgiven my father, but I'm not so sure that I did until much later. It's important to know that when we harbor feelings of resentment and anger toward someone else for their actions, we are really hurting ourselves. Life is precious, and holding a grudge is on the list of "not productive" things we can spend our time on. That grudge is heavy and quickly becomes a burden. It's kind of like building a snowman. You start by patting the grudge into a snowball in your hands, but then as you continue to roll it through the snow of life, the bigger it gets. The metaphor gets cheesier as I expand it by saying that you need to let the sun melt that snowball of grief, anger, and heartache. That warm sun is the love and grace of Jesus.

Maybe you are burdened by a giant snowball of resentment and feel like no matter the amount of sun, it will not melt. I urge you to let God into your life and you will soon feel His power to do marvelous works. Forgiveness is attainable.

Moment for Reflection

1.   How do you know if you've really forgiven a person?

2. What are some practical ways you can deal with feelings of resentment?

_____

_____

_____

_____

_____

3

A Living Faith

"Most likely to be a nun." I remember being so upset by this award that I didn't even show up for the yearbook picture.

In high school, I spent a lot of time showing others what it means to be a follower of Jesus. At a public high school, this is definitely not the norm. People did drugs and drank, and many of them were my friends and acquaintances, although I never participated in those shenanigans. My style wasn't super "in-your-face," but rather was more of a peaceful example of W.W.J.D. (What Would Jesus Do). Of course, I was not perfect and there were definitely times when my decisions were not the best, but overall, my friends knew where I stood when it came to eternity. I think that is ultimately why I got voted into the nun category, but it felt like somewhat of a mockery because a lot of what I stood for and tried to explain to people was that being a Christian is more about a relationship with Jesus than it is anything else. It's not about following rules and man-made traditions, or thinking you're perfect, or even that you need to be. It is about knowing that you are a sinner, admitting you need a savior (that's where Jesus comes in), and acknowledging that you cannot successfully live this life on your own. It's about opening your hands to receive God's free gifts of grace and forgiveness. It is as simple as that.

Please read this next part carefully (and go back and reread the previous part): God loves you so much that He gave His son Jesus as a sacrifice to die on a cross in order to forgive your sins so that you can spend eternity with Him. That is, undoubtedly, the most amazing truth you will ever hear. God loves you so much that He gave His son Jesus as a sacrifice to die on a cross in order to forgive your sins so that you can spend eternity with Him. I typed it again just in case you didn't catch the scope of it the first time. Dear reader, I pray that you have or will accept this information as truth and that you choose to accept Jesus as your savior if you haven't already. You are loved by the God of the universe. Let that sink in. If you've never accepted Jesus, but this truth rings true and you want to know the redemptive power of His love, pray this prayer now: Father, I know that I am a sinner. I acknowledge my need for a savior and know that I can find that in your son Jesus. I choose to receive your grace and follow you from this day forward. Thank you for your forgiveness and peace. Amen.

If you prayed this prayer, hallelujah! Please email me at sanddollarsandswisscheese@gmail.com and let me know so that I can rejoice with you!

If you have questions about this or want to discuss it further, please speak with a Christian you know, go talk to a pastor at a church, pick up a Bible and start reading, (may I suggest the gospel of John or the book of Romans?), and/or email me.

Wow, so I didn't plan on sharing the gospel so early in this book, but apparently that's where it needed to happen. Who knew that being voted as "most likely to be a nun" would turn into me preaching to others almost sixteen years later about how God can radically change your life for the better—hmmm—maybe they weren't so wrong about that nomination.

Joking aside, I am grateful that my witness in high school made people see me as a person who served Christ and His people. I strive to be that every day. The reason I was upset about it was because I want(ed) people to know that the Christian life is about authenticity, honesty, and dependence on a God who is bigger than you and me. It is not about a life of condemnation, ridicule, or violence which can sometimes be associated with "religion."

Looking back, the "we're just not sure" that I continually heard from doctors was a blessing of sorts. The disease had been there from the beginning, and although I had symptoms, I didn't receive an official diagnosis until later. I think if the doctors had figured out the puzzle sooner, my childhood would have been riddled with more anxiety and caution and less sports. That's part of why I carry such a fondness in my heart for my time as an athlete. The other part wasn't the competition, the practices, or even celebrating the wins; it was the people. My teammates were some of the best hearts around, and we had fun both on and off the field/court. Although my teammates made the bus rides memorable and the practices worth it, my coaches played a large role in developing the leader I am today, and for that I am sincerely grateful.

My freshman year on Varsity for softball, our assistant coach was a rockstar. Her endless positive attitude, desire to push us all to be our best selves (not just best athletes, but people too), and her ability to find the lesson in any situation made playing for her a privilege. At tryouts, she's the one that noticed I always snapped my ponytail forward as I watched the ball into my glove, which is what ultimately won my spot on the team. From that point forward, she encouraged us to snap our ponytails (thankfully I didn't yet know that I had a malformation in my skull, because if I had known, I'm sure I wouldn't have been doing any ponytail snapping). I admired her effectiveness at building relationships and creating an energetic environment, and when I reflect on who I am as a leader, I realize that I try to emulate her. She had the power to make every single one of us feel like we were the most important member of the team, while at the same time, emphasize the importance of working together to achieve our shared goals. Respectful leadership was a focus, and she modeled the tools that would ensure our success. If you're reading this Coach V., thanks for being you and for believing in me!

When I wasn't at practice or a game, I was either planning a school event or doing school work. I took several AP courses as a Junior and Senior and graduated as salutatorian of my class of over 370 students. Student council was also a big part of my high school life. I enjoyed influencing the happenings around school and continued through Junior year as class president and Senior year as co-president of Student Council. Planning all of those dances definitely prepared me for planning my wedding! One notable difference though, was that after spending weeks (sometimes months) planning for school dances, the let down at the end of the event was a bummer. I didn't get that feeling after my wedding because I was finally married to my best friend and about to embark on one of the best vacations to date (but I'll get to all of that later). I don't tell you all of this so you know how cool and nerdy I was in high school (ha ha), but rather to display the importance of being involved in the lives around you, and always doing and being your best.

The week before I graduated, one of my good friends asked if I wanted to go to Juarez, Mexico with her church. One of the trip attendees had dropped out, so they had an extra spot. Of course, I jumped at the invitation to practice my Spanish and spread the love of Christ. Although I had been a little nervous to attend because I only knew one person going, the trip left me rejuvenated, reflective, and ready for more service. The people I went with, the people from the other church that joined us, and those we served were such caring souls and it was a pleasure to spend a week with them. One of the lasting impressions I had from the trip that still affects me today was this: gratefulness is not dependent on your circumstances or your possessions, but rather, it acknowledges who God is and what He has done for His sons and daughters.

I met a lady at a worship service we held in the cafeteria where we were staying. She had six children and her youngest needed an eye surgery that she and her husband were unable to afford. In her complete dependence on the Lord, she came to the worship service to pray and ask for God's provision. I remember sitting with her as she cried (literally) out to Jesus in thanksgiving. Instead of asking for help, she thanked Him for all the blessings she had and was in awe of His ability to provide for His children. In comparison with me, she had so little in terms of creature comforts and financial security, but yet she was focusing on what she did have. What a challenge to us as we reflect on what we have and choose to dwell on God's continued faithfulness rather than our wants (or needs in this case).

> Remember that gratefulness is not dependent on your circumstances or your possessions, but rather, it acknowledges who God is and what He has done for you.

Later that summer, I attended a Christian leadership conference in Tennessee with a good friend from church. We were really enjoying the speakers, the people, and the warm weather, but I soon found myself sick in bed (remember that issue of easily getting dehydrated?). Since I was so far from home, I had no choice but to go to the ER. At that point, I couldn't keep any food down and hadn't gotten out of bed for a good twenty four hours due to a horrible migraine. I remember the ER doctor was very rude and had made me promise him more than once that I wasn't pregnant. He gave me some anti-nausea medication, and something for the pain, but insisted there wasn't much else he could do. The conference ended, and my friend's parents came to drive us home. A ten-hour road trip in a minivan in July is probably the last thing I wanted to be doing, but I was just happy to be going home.

Once home though, I spent the next four days in and out of a migraine haze. Thinking back, I'm not sure why my mom hadn't decided to bring me to the hospital. I've blocked most of that time out of my memory, but not going to the hospital was probably due to me begging her not to take me. By the grace of God and as an answer to many prayers, I recovered from what I'm sure was my second case of undiagnosed aseptic meningitis. Essentially, my meninges, which comprise the tissue lining around my brain, were most likely swollen due to a disease that I still didn't know I had. The aseptic part just means that it wasn't necessarily caused by any infection like typical meningitis, but just due to the disease process. They say hindsight is 20/20. You too will see more clearly as this story continues.

As I remember the day I could finally lift my head from the pillow without feeling like I was teetering at the pinnacle of Mt. Everest, I see bright sunlight. I would chalk that up to a miracle right there. I don't really remember the four days in bed, nauseous and vomiting, or the week before that I spent in the grueling hot weather of Tennessee in a dorm room bed with similar symptoms.

Do you have any memories of a terrible event in your life that when you think back, you only remember the good? Have you experienced a loss of a family member or friend, but instead of remembering the pain that loss caused, you think of all of the happy times you had with them? When you think about some of the tragedies our country has experienced, do you remember the helpers—the people who came together to overcome adversity? I am so very grateful that I'm not good at remembering the bad stuff.

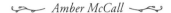

I remember the people who helped me, cared for me, and prayed for me, and I thank God for that. Granted, there are some tough memories I have that aren't fun to look back on, but even still, I know the memory is much less threatening than the actual events.

REMEMBER
the things
I HAVE DONE
in the past.
FOR I ALONE
Am god

Isaiah 46:9
NLT

Memories

I love looking back and remembering the good times. My husband gawks at the 8,000+ photos I have on my phone and doesn't understand why I can't transfer the old ones to the computer. It's because once they get transferred to the hard drive, I rarely look at them. The accessibility factor is high when they are just in my phone's photo album, and I often look at them and reminisce. It's not a longing for times gone by, just a celebration of those times. I am still very grateful for where I am today, so having those memories doesn't keep me in the past, but instead reminds me where I've been.

Finding time to preserve memories in a fun way can be difficult. As I've gotten older, I find that I have less and less "free time" to scrapbook like I used to. It's such a bummer, because I really enjoy admiring my old scrapbooks! I would like to start setting apart some time each month to document memories, and I encourage you to do something similar if it's important to you! I have also found that a five year journal (one line a day) has helped me jot down quick memories.

My memory isn't as good as it once was, so I need to be more diligent about preserving the special moments. One thing I don't mind about my worsening memory is that it is pretty ineffective at remembering the bad stuff. I encourage you to try to weed out negative memories as much as possible by surrendering them in prayer. God can take our thoughts captive if we let Him, and He actually asks us to do just that in 2 Corinthians 10:5.

Moment for Reflection

1. Think of a moment that brought you joy this week that you would like to remember. Take a few minutes to jot it down.

_____

_____

_____

_____

_____

2. Are there ways you are intentionally taking time to remember happy things from your past? If not, how could you incorporate this into your life?

_____

_____

_____

_____

_____

4

New Friends

Man, I loved college!

I met my college roommate over the phone, and we discussed the important things like who was going to bring the t.v. and our favorite snack foods. Little did I know, I was talking about living arrangements with my soon-to-be best friend. Although SBB was afraid of balls, including volleyballs, softballs, basketballs and the like, we had a similar sense of humor and our work ethics were ambitious. We worked hard and played hard (not volleyball–at least not together). People thought we were so weird when we lofted both of our beds and slept side-by-side every night, but we thought nothing could be more normal. One day, SBB told me she felt like we were an old married couple because she always had to remind me about my meds. See, the migraines that sentenced me to days in the nurse's office had never really left. I was dependent on Excedrin Migraine and on many occasions found myself missing out on fun due to the latest attack.

Find your people. The ones who will graciously remind you about your meds, but also help you feel normal and welcome even when you're feeling sick.

March of 2007 was littered with daily migraines, but also extreme jaw pain, to the point of not being able to chew food. The oral surgeon determined I needed my wisdom teeth out, so the operation was scheduled for May. The morning of the surgery, the surgeon did a precautionary panoramic x-ray and found that I had a one-and-a-half-inch cyst on the left side of my bottom jaw. Thankfully, he was able to remove what was there and informed me that my jaw was so thin that "any longer and you would've had to have reconstructive jaw surgery."

The next three weeks were terrible. I had major dry sockets and couldn't really eat anything other than applesauce and soft ice cream (okay, so not THAT terrible). The dry socket where the cyst had been was the worst one and took even longer than normal to heal. During this time, I also discovered that I react adversely to codeine, and to this day, I refuse to take any type of narcotic.

Communicate your experience with your medication. Not all medicine is going to work the same for each patient. If it's not working, stop taking it.

Despite the constant toothache, I was loving my classes and making new friends. One of those classes was a media/communication class that I took on Monday nights. At a liberal arts college, you take a variety of courses outside your major to "discover" other interests. It's not hippie-dippie, at least it wasn't at Carthage. So, I found myself in a night class as the only freshman—talk about intimidating! I remember the first night; I sat at a desk near the door since I was one of the last students to arrive. Shortly after me, a boy walked in and sat, leaving one desk between us. I didn't say much that night and left right when class was over. The next day, I was at Intervarsity Christian Fellowship, which is a national Christian group that meets on college campuses to hear a message about Jesus and worship through music. The boy from my night class was there, so SBB and I went over to say hi. He had a goofy grin, brown, fluffy (in a cute way) hair, and I could tell by his hand gestures that he was a good storyteller (and probably Italian). We became fast friends.

The next week, the boy from class, Chris, walked back to the dorms with me after night class and I learned that he made waffles for his floor (he was a resident assistant), which I thought was so strange. Like, a bunch of guys just wanted to eat waffles?! Weird, but I'm pretty sure he bought a waffle maker just to keep them happy. Whatever it takes, I guess! It was then that I first realized how much he cared about other people.

SBB and I also spent a lot of time with a tall, skinny boy who loved to wear the hood up on his sweatshirts, who we called "Habitat boy," because SBB and some of our other friends met him in their Habitat for Humanity group. So, Chris, Habitat boy (HB), SBB, and I hung out often.

There were numerous pranks played between the four of us. For example, one time I saved up all of the paper hole punches from the library (Chris worked there, so we visited the desk often) in a Folgers coffee can and the day before winter break ran into their dorm yelling, "It's snowing!" while tossing the "flakes" into the air. Ha! They were so upset!

Chris and HB were tired of being outwitted and outmaneuvered and felt they needed to strike back! In true ninja form, they waited several weeks after our most recent prank. Chris told SBB and I at lunch that there was something we needed to discuss that night and asked us to meet him and HB behind the TWC (a building on campus). Innocently, we thought there was actually something to discuss, so we headed over there around 8:30 as requested. It was a super soaker attack—we immediately regretted our decision as we high-tailed it for safety!

One of the most clever things that HB and Chris did was create an amazing scavenger hunt for us. I remember the clues being fairly genius and pretty difficult. They had us all over campus for hours—we even had to fish out a clue from a plastic coke bottle with a rock in the bottom, tied to a string and hidden in the creek. I wish I had kept a copy of the clues! Anyway, after all that effort, we were hoping the prize was something worthwhile. To our dismay, the last clue led us underneath the step on the binoculars overlooking Lake Michigan, to find Santa undies that had originally been found in the ceiling of one of the other guys' dorms. Come onnnnnnnn. At least they were in a Ziploc bag so we could conveniently throw them in the garbage right after we found them, but what a lame ending to an epic hunt!

The summer of 2007, I headed to the upper peninsula of Michigan. Our Intervarsity chapter had their annual retreat up there, and I was excited to spend the weekend digging into God's word, singing hymns by the campfire, and learning how to sail. The week included all of those things, as well as seeing otters holding hands (are you serious with that cuteness?) in Lake Superior, and hearing God call me to be a small group Bible study leader for the following school year.

The truth is, I didn't want to do it. I was scared and felt extremely unprepared. It reminds me of the story in Exodus, when God spoke to Moses and commanded him to go to Egypt (the place where he was raised) and demand that Ramses (his adopted brother who he hadn't seen in forty-plus years) set God's people (the Israelites) free. If you're not familiar with the story, Moses was born an Israelite during a time in which the Pharaoh declared that all Israelite male babies be killed. The Israelites were slaves, and when Moses's mother had him, she protected him in hiding. She then sent him in a basket down the Nile. You may think she was pretty brave and VERY reckless, if you don't realize that she trusted that God would provide for her son. Thankfully, God used her faithfulness to (spoiler alert) save the Israelites from slavery many years later.

I encourage you to read the story to see how God took an unlikely leader and prepared Moses to do exactly what God needed him to do. Now, I realize the difference in scale between leading the entire nation of Israel and leading a small group of college students for a semester, but both have their importance. I prayed about my lack of confidence, and God soon revealed that it didn't matter if I knew all the answers or if I was able to quote a ton of scripture. It mattered that I was committed to guiding these freshmen through life, utilizing our most powerful tools: prayer and the Bible. It wasn't about what *I* could or couldn't do, but ultimately about whether or not I was willing and ready to rely fully on God in order to complete His will. Thankfully, I chose to submit to His call and co-led a group of about ten freshmen during my sophomore year.

It was such a rewarding experience, and I discovered a passion for biblical ministry and leadership that I hadn't explored before. This led me to co-leading a small group during the fall semester of my Junior year with Chris. We were very good friends by that point, and working as a team was very natural. The moments we had within that small group were fun, focused on the word of God, and definitely brought healing to some of the souls in that group. Our backgrounds were varied, but God used that semester to bring us all closer as brothers and sisters in Christ. We shared our lives–the fears, the hopes, the dreams, and everything in between. It was a true picture of how we should relate as children of God. Without taking the first step and trusting God to speak through me as a small group leader, I would've missed these opportunities, and I'm so thankful I took that step.

Chris and I had a very platonic relationship. We were both dating other people at the time, and our friendship, in no way, hindered our romantic relationships. I had been happily dating my high school sweetheart and had even picked out a ring! Chris was dating a girl a year older than him who had chosen to teach abroad when she graduated, so she was in Korea his senior year. If you know me, you know where this is going, but at the time, neither of us had any idea! Apparently our friends saw it long before we did. Now, if you don't know me, you're probably picking up on the fact that something wild is about to happen. You would be right. Lots of wild things happened, beginning in December of 2008.

I was scheduled to leave for a semester in Guatemala on the 3rd of January, 2009. My emotions were mixed. I had planned to return to that beautiful country (after spending January of 2008 there on a J-term trip) to teach in the village I was going to live in and take classes at a local university. That was all very exciting, but leaving my friends, my comfort zone, and my first language for six months was a little scary. For the moment though, I had other things to consider.

Chris and I were enjoying a planning dinner for our last small group before I was to leave for Guatemala. For all of my fellow Carthage grads, we were sitting in Einstein's probably eating a Tasty Turkey and a bagel dog. Near the end of our dinner, Chris said, "So, HB asked me a question the other day. *no pause* He asked me if you and I would be dating if we weren't dating other people."

long pause

I looked at him, rather shocked by the words that I had just heard come out of his mouth.

"I said yes."

Wow, well, now I really didn't know what to say. To be honest, I don't remember exactly what I *did* say. I probably laughed awkwardly and said, "No, you didn't!"

I do remember walking back to the dorms after that and somehow feeling like something had changed. I remember talking about the fact that I was leaving, was practically engaged to someone else, and how anything other than what we had just wasn't really possible. I had never seen him as more than a friend, and it wasn't going to change. We laughed off the conversation we had just had and chalked it up to us just being such great friends that of course people wondered if it could lead to something more. I was thankful to be leaving on a jet plane in a week so that I could process his answer in peace.

We can make
our plans
but the LORD
DETERMINES
our steps

Proverbs 16:9
NLT

Expect the Unexpected

Some of us are planners by nature. I, for one, am mostly Type A. At least when it comes to organization and big life decisions. I felt so good about the relationship I was in and the fact that my boyfriend was making payments on a ring. I loved him.

As I get older, I am less and less Type A and more and more Type "God is in control, I will pray for His guidance and for His will to be done." That doesn't look as clean on a personality vitae, but that is the reality of living a life where time and time again God shows up in the most amazing ways and shows you that your plans are not the best. He continues to remind me that He knows my heart, He knows the future, and He will guide me along the way if I let Him. If I don't surrender the control, the process is more difficult and will probably take a lot longer.

Ultimately, none of us are really in control anyway. Yes, we have free will and the ability to choose our own path, but when you stop and think about that for just a second, you realize that trusting the God of the universe with your life is a "no duh" choice versus trusting yourself.

God has big plans for you if you will just take His hand. You will hear more about Chris throughout the rest of this book, and as you do, will realize just how much better God's plans are.

Moment for Reflection

1. What is something you have been struggling to trust God with?

    _____

    _____

    _____

    _____

a. What would surrendering that to Him look like?

_____

_____

_____

_____

_____

5

Living Alone

I was excited that I had finally moved into the house I would be living in for the next five months. Starting by cleaning the fridge seemed like a good idea, so I opened the door and realized I wasn't alone as a frog jumped from the top shelf and a cockroach fell from a lower one and landed on his back. Once I regained my composure, I kicked him gently with my foot to flip him over, as I came to the realization that this semester may push me well past my comfort zone in more than one way. Over the next five and a half months, I would see that I was more right than I probably wanted to be.

Let me back up a bit. I mentioned in the previous chapter that I was spending the second semester of my junior year in Guatemala. The year before, I had spent three weeks there falling in love with the beautiful landscape, delicious food, and wonderfully kind-hearted people. I loved it so much that I decided to exchange my Chemistry major for a Spanish one and travel back the following year to fulfill my study-abroad requirement. I had heard plenty of stories of students "partying abroad" rather than actually going to a new country with intentionality and purpose, and I wanted to ensure that wasn't how I would be spending my time. I worked closely with my professor to create an experience that would be meaningful and worthwhile.

It worked out nicely that the English teacher from the community

I would be living in, *Nuevo Horizonte* (New Horizon), was getting his degree at this time and chose to study in Canada. While he was gone, the high school would need a new English teacher, so I offered to fill the role. Ironically, he was also the science teacher, so I found myself teaching Physics and Chemistry as well. I ventured down there with no classes or teacher training, armed only with a Spanish Chemistry book that my high school Chem teacher graciously offered me when I reached out in desperation.

I traveled that January with a group of students from my college and two professors who shared their knowledge of the Guatemalan Civil War and agricultural economics with us as we traversed the beautiful mountains, black sand beaches, and crystal blue waters of *Lago de Atitlán*. The previous year, my trip to the lake was a rude awakening to Guatemalan transportation. Our group of about thirty students boarded a *chicken bus,* a school bus that had been decorated in bright colorful paintings and now hosted chickens and their owners traveling to their next destination instead of school children. The bus, driven by one of the bravest Guatemala has to offer, sped up and down the one-lane mountain road in the dark. The lack of guardrails made passing oncoming vehicles seemingly life-threatening.

Our safe arrival had us collectively exhaling the breath we had been holding for the last hour and a half. With that experience as a not-so-distant memory, I found myself a year later on my way to the consulate to take care of the necessary paperwork to make my six-month stay possible. I wasn't in a chicken bus this time, but rather a taxi cab with a driver who was supposedly trustworthy, according to our friendly hostel owners (who my professor knew well). I navigated my way through the consulate *solita* and found the cab driver waiting for me in the hot sun.

The sweat trickling down the back of my neck wasn't just due to the missing air conditioning. Ruiz's route didn't look anything like the trip I had made just twelve months prior. Although the road was just as narrow, the landscape was drastically different. We were on rather flat land for the first half of the trip, and my normally positive thoughts headed down a scary path. Was he actually taking me to the lake? If not, how long would it take the group to realize I was missing? Even if they did, would they be able to track down this murderer? Even worse, we hadn't said a word in over an hour.

I am not sure of the exact words I was praying, but they probably sounded something like "Jesus, take the wheel," as we drove closer to what seemed to be my demise. I was clinging to those prayers like a lifeline when I noticed a small plastic card sticking out of Ruiz's visor. The familiar Catholic portrayal of the Virgin Mary peered at me from behind other nondescript colorful pieces of paper. I was overwhelmingly grateful for that card that gave me the opportunity to ask about his faith. Our discussion comforted us both and made further, random conversation possible. Shortly, we made it to the base of the mountain, which I determined was just the back side of it, and dangerously zigzagged to the boat launch that I recognized from my earlier trip. Praise Jesus!

I thanked Ruiz and said my goodbyes, extremely grateful that his imagined reputation as a murderer was far from my mind. The next few days at the lake were marvelous as we explored the mountain paths by foot and glided over the water in *lanchas* to the other villages around the sunken volcano. My admiration for the people and culture grew on one particular path when we had to graciously pass some slow-moving women. The reason for their labored movement was the enormous bags of coffee beans that they had strapped to their heads and were carrying on their backs. I am not a coffee drinker, but if you are, be reminded of the toil that helped bring you that gross bean water the next time you take a sip.

This life-changing experience would not have been possible without the help and insight my Spanish professor offered as we planned that trip. The opportunity to work as a teacher in the community was such a blessing and prepared me significantly for other teaching experiences I would have once I returned to the States. It was helpful that I worked with the same students teaching both English and Science, because I could support them in their development of English as they supported me by teaching me words like *arco iris* (rainbow) and *los nombres de los elementos en la tabla periódica* (the names of the elements in the periodic table).

There were about four hundred people who "did life" together as socialists in the village. Not in the way that we think about socialism as Americans or as it has been experimented with in some countries, but in the pure sense of the word. The Acts 2 sense of the word where everyone looks out for everyone else, you grow or buy your own food, but if your neighbor needs some, you give it to them. I think life is still done this way in many parts of the world, and just because we don't always see "love your neighbor" on the 5:00 news, in our seemingly closed-off, barely-smile-at-strangers-let-alone-give-them-the-shirt-off-my-back society we live in in the United States, I'm convinced there is still genuine neighborly love out there, especially where you look for it. God created us for community; it's how it was meant to be. I will say that I don't think this type of socialism is sustainable or even possible at a large scale.

Anyway, I'm making it sound *really* good there and *pretty* bad here. I'm being a little dramatic. Although I loved the community I lived in, it wasn't free of problems. Namely, the tarantulas. I mean, *come on* with these things! Even the spiders that weren't technically tarantulas were *gigantescas*, and I wanted nothing to do with them—especially not when they spent the night in my bed. If you don't already know this about me, let me tell you something: I am an arachnophobe to the max. How I ever survived in a country where spiders are more like something out of *The Lord of the Rings* movies is beyond my scope of comprehension–I mean, honestly, only by the grace of God and the machete skills of my neighbor boys. Honestly.

Not only did I have huge spiders living in my house, I also had a two-foot iguana living in my back room upon my arrival. He only stayed a few days and then vacated the premises of his own accord. It probably would've been nice to have him hang around to eat all the mosquitos. At any given moment I had at least three hundred mosquito bites, and somehow I made it out with no malaria and no West Nile virus. Ironically, during my time in Guatemala, the swine flu was running rampant in the U.S., so thankfully, I avoided that too!

Outside my bedroom window (which of course had no glass or screen and was basically just three pieces of wood somewhat nailed together) there lived a swarm of African black bees that built a lovely home for themselves over several months. The science/nature nerd in me thought it was really cool to watch as the hive grew a little bigger each day, so I documented the progress with photographs and thankfully never had any too-close encounters with the dangerous torpedos with wings.

I had a few other friends that visited daily, including the rooster and hens that walked freely through my home. How did they get in the door, you ask? Oh, don't be silly. I didn't have a door. My house was made of cement blocks and a roof that wasn't strong enough to withstand the "houseplant" that grew right through it. I had a nice, airy, open courtyard that was home to my hammock (because everyone has a napping hammock in Guate), my kitchen, and the dining area. The open courtyard continued to the backyard where you could walk twenty feet to get to the outhouse. Before we get to that though, let's finish with the attached structure. To the left of the kitchen, which did have a stove (that worked most days) as well as a refrigerator (you know, the one with the frog and cockroach), was my spa. Now, this is probably not like any spa you've ever been to.

It did have three walls, but they didn't go all the way to the ground (think bathroom stall-esque), and a roof. It also had a *pila* (sink), as well as a garden hose attached to the spigot. The hose worked nicely as a shower when draped over a string I tied from one side of the room to the other. This is how I showered almost every day for six months. One thing that might stop the pity party you are throwing in your head for me is that it was at least 95 degrees every day, so the fact that I had to shower with freezing cold hose water wasn't all that terrible.

My bedroom was on the opposite side of the house. Thankfully, this room had four walls and a door that locked. It was very spacious, with a small dresser, a barely-twin-sized bed, and a small night stand where I kept my mirror propped up—until the day I went to pick it up and found a three-and-a-half-inch spider on the other side. You guys, no joke, I don't know how I survived! Remember those machete-wielding neighbor boys I told you about? One night I had to go get them because there was a spider in my bed. *In.my.bed.* Gah. Alright, I think I'll only talk about spiders one or two more times–just to get the point across that I'm basically a saint for living there for as long as I did with all of those nasty creatures. I forgot the most important thing in my room: a mosquito net. I used it diligently for a while, but it started feeling less like one of those princess veil beds and more like a stuffy trap, so I stopped. The CDC (or whatever they call it in Guatemala) sprayed for mosquitos twice in the six months that I lived there (which led to me returning home one day to find a dying tarantula–I barely made it three sentences–on one of my shoes and calling for the neighbor boys again!) and no malaria, so the moral of the story: I didn't need the mosquito net.

Okay, back to the outhouse. It was a crumbling cement structure in the middle of my backyard that had half a door, a cockroach family and eighty seven of their closest friends living in it, and no toilet seat. I'm all about living within my means and really becoming part of the culture, and I could handle (somewhat) the garden hose and bucket showers, but I was not up for this. Especially since my intestines couldn't really keep up with my new environment and I was spending more time in the bathroom than I cared to. I used the bathroom in *el albergue* for awhile, which was somewhat of a dorm room where eco-tourists stayed (I'll get to them in a little bit), but that was at least half a block away, and when nature calls, sometimes you don't have half a block's time. You just don't.

I quickly (like within a day or two of taking up residence in my new house) had a conversation with the president of the community and worked out a plan for building a bathroom at my house that had a flushable toilet—one with a seat even! Woah, dream big, amiright?!

We are already **seventeen** paragraphs into the chapter, and I've barely just begun describing my new digs to you! It's just really important that you understand how much of an adjustment it was for me and how spoiled I was in the States with my enclosed hot water shower, a house with a front door, a home (mostly) free of animals and insects, and **air conditioning**. I was somewhat miserable for the first few months I was there. Although I was loving teaching, I was doing a pretty terrible job of putting myself out there, meaning I spent most of my nights alone. I would take my laptop and my internet stick, which I paid several pretty *quetzales* (Guatemalan currency) for every month, and hike up to the top of the tower that was in the center of the community so I could get a signal that allowed me to talk to friends and family back home. I was lonely (maybe a little depressed) and doing a good job of staying connected to home as an excuse not to "impose" on the families I was living amongst.

Not only was I teaching at the community's high school, I was taking junior-level psychology courses at *La Universidad de Santa Elena*. The first weekend after the students and professors from

Carthage left the village (they were only there for about two weeks), I started class in the city. Friday night, before class, I got very sick. I mean, we are talking about out-of-both-ends-don't-know-where-those-noises-are-coming-from sickness. Yes, very sick. At this point, I didn't have my relationships established with my village mamas who eventually had my back, so I was virtually on my own. Thankfully, I was still in *el albergue* at this point, so I had a flushing toilet. I spent the night praying that I would be able to stand up in the morning, get on the crowded *micro* (essentially a fifteen-passenger van that they stuffed no less than twenty people into), make my way into Santa Elena, to then hail a tiny taxi called a *tuk tuk*, and make the speedy, bumpy three-mile trip to the university. That's exactly what I did Saturday morning as I woke in a haze of stomach cramps and headache.

Surprisingly, I survived the trip that I would take every weekend for the next five months and was the first to show up to class. Soon, a skinny Guatemalan girl with a huge smile sat down next to me and asked me my name. She then asked me a lot more questions, and I asked her a few. Little did I know, I was meeting my Guatemalan best friend. Izzy and I fell in step together, and after class she invited me to her house. At this point, I hadn't eaten in close to thirty six hours and just wanted to sleep after five hours of class, so I thanked her for the invite, offered my apologies, and told her we'd catch up next week.

Well, the next Saturday came. I decided she was nice enough and probably wouldn't drive me into the mountains to leave me for dead (things had worked out alright with that cab driver!), so I took the chance and got into her car after class. That was one of the best decisions I made in those six months.

Izzy's family was just as likable and smiley as she was (except her dad, but his silent stoicism was a mask covering a long, hard life and a tender heart). I was still extremely homesick and out of my comfort zone, so when I realized they had (luke)warm water and a private shower, I knew we'd be friends forever. I'm joking—I loved them for their jovial personalities, kind hearts, generosity, *and* their shower. The weekends became my time in the city with the Masa family. We shopped, dined at all the best restaurants that Santa Elena had to offer, and even took the occasional trip to the beach or into the mountains to swim in the *Lago Petén Itzá*. We had a blast going to the circus and having candy apples, dancing the night away at a few family weddings, and driving to watch Izzy's boyfriend race in dirt bike competitions. I am so grateful for, and overwhelmed by, the way the Masa family embraced me as one of their own without knowing much about me.

It wasn't all fun and games. Living without air conditioning and sweating through my clothes multiple times a day meant that I often had migraines. One Sunday, we visited a Masa relative a couple of hours from Santa Elena. On the long car ride, I started feeling sick and went to grab my medicine. To my dismay, my coin purse was empty! Izzy noticed my concern and we detoured to the nearest pharmacy. This wasn't Walgreens or CVS, but rather a small window shop run out of someone's home. Unfortunately, those people were *not* home, so we had to find somewhere else. The next one was open and thankfully had what I needed. Although it may seem super sketchy to be buying and taking medicine at a "home" pharmacy, it's just how things are done there—especially in the countryside. Thankfully, my disease didn't flare up as much as I was anticipating—I had whispered many prayers before and during that trip that I would stay healthy.

> Take all of your medicines with you when traveling, and have a plan in place with your doctor as to what would happen if you were to need medical support on the trip.

A couple months into my stay, I was feeling the pull to city life with the Masa family, which afforded a few of the creature comforts I remembered from home (remember that warm shower?). To add a dimension to it, there was somewhat of a stigma about the village I was living in. Guatemala had a thirty-six-year civil war, and the village's inhabitants were guerrilla fighters that combated the Guatemalan government. They were real-life warriors who had called the jungle their home for many years. My classmates in Santa Elena, including Izzy and her family, knew only what the government propaganda had portrayed of the guerrilla fighters. Essentially, they were afraid of the guerillas and often asked how I could live with such horrible monsters. I was shunned in my Guatemalan culture class for trying to defend those whom I had come to know and love.

I had also made some enemies in my behavioral statistics class. Apparently, "cheating" isn't seen the same way as it is in the States, and when I refused to help my classmates during the statistics exams (with the professor sitting right in the room, mind you), I was ridiculed and demeaned. I was made to feel like a traitor when I was just doing what I thought was the right thing, what I had been raised to do. Talk about culture shock. It is such a strange moment when two worldviews collide and you find yourself trapped in the middle. I didn't offer any answers and managed to pass the exam with an A, despite the pressure from both my peers and my professor.

Not all my classes were so torturous. Neurophysiology is fascinating no matter the language you study it in. Thankfully, I survived on lots of re-reading and cognates (thank you science, for using latin-based roots). My group project on the brain went off without a hitch, and my love for learning about how God designed us increased dramatically. My professor was brilliant and had no qualms about challenging us to memorize the inner workings of the human brain.

About halfway through my stay, my mom was planning to visit me and take a trip to the South for *Semana Santa* (Holy Week). She called me about a week before she was scheduled to arrive and was desperately explaining how dangerous Guatemala was and how the state website discouraged people from visiting.

"Mom, I live here. I promise that the area I'm in is safe." I reassured her, as I pushed the sound of the *narcotraficante* planes out of my head. Despite living next to a known drug trafficking farm, El Petén (the northern region of Guatemala where I was living) *was* relatively safe. My convincing worked, and she showed up on time. To be fair, my mom's worries weren't unwarranted. She is a five-foot-seven blonde-haired, blue-eyed woman who doesn't speak more than "hola! Como es-tas?" I'm actually really proud of her for making her way through the Guatemala City airport and on to me two hours later. I'm sure navigating a country where you don't speak the language is terrifying, and I'm not sure that I'm that brave!

She was finally there, and for the next week, I didn't have to think about how I was lonely, dreading the end of every weekend, and not sure I was going to make it another two and a half months.

"You've gained almost twenty five pounds!" greeted my mother as she stepped off the airplane. Okay, maybe not THAT immediate, but it didn't make me feel better that she had waited a few minutes. So I had overindulged in homemade corn tortillas for the first half of my stay. You would too if you were to try them! Due to her motherly greeting, I determined I would take up running the day my mom left.

Our first leg of the trip started with a twelve-hour, overnight, bus ride to *Lago de Atitlán*. If you've never been, google it. It is one of the most beautiful places I've ever been, and I was excited to be going back for the third time. First though, we had to take a dreadful bus trip. My mom was already apprehensive (remember the state website warnings), and to make matters worse, they had chosen the worst possible movie to play for us. I don't know the name of it, but let me just explain the plot a bit. Some tourists are traveling in a foreign country on a bus, and then motorcycle terrorists start following them. The bus driver stops and abandons ship and the tourists are left to fight off the terrorists in a firefight in a junkyard. Splendid! Now all of the images dancing in our minds were playing on the screen in front of us. Thankfully, that's all we saw of them, as we made it safely to Guatemala City and jumped in a cab with a sweet driver who drove us the two hours to the lake.

We shopped for treasures and trinkets and ate the freshest fish I've ever had. A festival lined the streets every day in celebration of *Semana Santa*, so we enjoyed lots of live music and dancing. Long motor boats transported us to lively little towns around the lake, each displaying their pride and honor in the colorful streets decorated with flags and banners as they celebrated the week leading to Easter. After a few days eating and drinking Guatemala's finest, we boarded another bus that took us to a Spanish-baroque style town called Antigua.

Our adventure had taken a turn for the wilder side as we awoke early the next morning to hike Mount Pacaya. You see, Mt. Pacaya is an active volcano. If you don't know, some active volcanoes are covered in lava rock. My mom and I trudged up the volcano over lots of lava rock wearing Keen sandals, which, if you aren't familiar, are strappy and have plenty of room for grinding rock to get inside. Standing five feet from a live lava flow was pretty spectacular, and I had the feet of a street urchin to show for it. My bath that night was gloriously relaxing and the water was filthy. The rest of our time there involved Spanish cathedrals, some amazing ruins from a years-old volcanic eruption, and more good food.

Leg three of the trip brought us over the Guatemalan border into Belize. Our accommodations on the way into the country reminded me of summer camp. Tiny cabins spotted the luscious green hillside and were home to scorpions and many other fun cabin mates. The saving grace of that camp was the butterfly house which housed thousands of friendly flutterers.

I remember spending one morning on the bank of the river playing cribbage and meeting some mischievous kiddos. They taught us how to catch iguanas, the success of which meant they would eat their next meal. If you caught a pregnant one, it meant you also had breakfast the next morning. We thanked them for the lesson, accepted their dinner invitation, and then voyaged on a ferry to the other side of the river to spend some time trekking through history in the nearby Maya ruins. The precision and accuracy of the mathematics those people must've understood amazes me.

Dinner was thankfully not iguana, nor iguana eggs. It was up the hill into the village, past the local church, at a small cafe. Walking through town, we tried to imagine what it had been like before Coca-Cola and the Bimbo company had pasted their signs everywhere. The children shared what history they had heard from their parents and were gracious hosts. Meeting people while traveling and learning their daily routines and cultural decisions is so energizing.

Day three in Belize led us just outside San Ignacio to the Actun Tunichil Muknal cave, which is understandably dubbed "ATM". Our Belizean tour guide was thoughtful, witty, and musically talented as he shared the history and local folklore that had been passed down from generation to generation. His musical talent shined through as he "played" some stalactites that had been around for centuries. In many of the caverns, we saw left-behind pottery and even skeletal remains of the humans that had once called this cave home. Exploring a space like that, pondering what had happened millenia ago is humbling and intriguing. It puts your life into the timeline of human history and helps you realize the enormity of being such a tiny part of existence.

Upon our return to Guatemala, I introduced my mom to the Masa family and we spent the day at Tikal, one of the largest sites of ruins from the Maya civilization. Again, inspiring, informative, and made us feel so insignificant. The howler and spider monkeys traipse and swing through the canopy, and you almost feel like they are watching you (which is confirmed when the spider monkeys stop and throw their poop at you!). On the other end of the spectrum, you see the carpenter ants forming a long black line spotted with green. Those little machines cut more leaves before big rainstorms and therefore are often a predictor for rain used by the locals. Howler monkeys also tend to howl more loudly right before a storm, which I found to be very true living next to a couple families that tended to be right more often than not.

Thankfully, I had the opportunity to show my mom around the village. We even took a hike through the jungle, and upon our return, were scolded by the village president. He was upset that we had gone into the jungle alone and was overjoyed that we hadn't encountered any jaguars during our trip. He warned me about how others had been followed by the lurking green eyes. You know what they say, "ignorance is bliss!" Had we heard his warnings before our two-hour hike, we probably would've reconsidered!

My mom left at the end of our amazing, fun-filled, nine-day trip with lots of hugs and a long conversation about how I needed to spend more time with families in the village and not feel like I was intruding. So, that's exactly what I did. I stepped out of my comfort zone and directly into the homes of the families I had been living amongst (but not really *with*) for the last few months. This push from my mom was exactly what I needed to get out of my funk, and thankfully, it came at exactly the right time.

Things back home were not going very well.

Due to some circumstances, which I will not describe here, my boyfriend and I ended our five-year relationship on the eve of my 21st birthday. I was crushed and alone, almost 3,000 miles from home. Thankfully, I had heeded my mother's advice to cultivate relationships and therefore had several families that wanted to celebrate my big day with me.

By the time the Masa family asked me to come to Santa Elena midweek to celebrate my birthday, I had already agreed to dinner with the Tono family. I spoke with Maria to see if she would agree to my plan. Thankfully, she was optimistic, and all of us spent the evening together at Maria's house. Due to all of the brainwashing and preconceived notions held by the Masa family about the villagers, I was shocked, but thrilled that they had agreed to come. Maria had made the most delicious *mole (moh-lay)* and I blew out the candles on TWO birthday cakes. My Guatemalan families had finally met and were getting along swimmingly. The festivities of the evening practically made me forget about the collapse of my relationship back home, and I was grateful for that.

I treasure the photo we took together at the end of the evening. Even more, I treasure the words that Mama Masa spoke to me before she left. She exclaimed that coming was a great idea, despite her uncertainty about it at the beginning of the evening, and that she no longer feared the village. I'd call that a win!

The last few weeks of my time in Guatemala were the best ones! I was finally eating meals with families in the village, and my desire to be in town all the time flipped to a preference of spending time in NH. The bugs, dust, and bucket showers were my new normal. I still used my flushing toilet and avoided the spiders at all costs (I wasn't dumb!), but everything else just wasn't a big deal anymore. I valued the human relationships over the creature and commercial comforts, and I was sad I would soon be heading home.

My sister (another blonde-haired, blue-eyed, beauty with no Spanish) bravely made her way to the jungle the last week I was there. She met all of my new friends, and all the teenage boys gawked over her. We cleaned up my house, packed my belongings, and dispersed all of my shoes to the neighborhood kids. I said *hasta la próxima* to my students and all of my new family members. It was such a bittersweet time, and I am glad my sister was there to guide me through the haze of leaving this place I had come to love.

Be thankful
in all
circumstances,
for this is
God's will
for you
who belong
to Christ
Jesus

1 Thessalonians
5:18
NLT

Appreciating the little things

If you've ever talked to someone after a mission trip they've taken to a third world country, I'm sure you've heard them describe the "lack" that is so evident. My time in Guatemala showed me the importance of appreciating (and celebrating) the little things. Ultimately, it doesn't matter if you don't have hot water to shower with (and yes, even in 100 degree weather, it is sometimes difficult to shower in freezing cold water) or there are bugs everywhere; what matters is the people: the memories you make, the relationships you build, and the support and love you share with them. It's the early morning jungle hike where you track a group of howlers or the freshest pineapple you've ever eaten because it came straight from the plant. It's spending time going to the *molina* to ground corn and then spending a few hours with your Guatemalan mama (one of them) learning how to make tortillas that taste better than any you can find in the States. It's your neighbor boys coming over to cut your grass with machetes or kill the latest eight-legged invader. It's visiting one of your faves to have a nice chat while she lets you use her washing machine to clean your sweat-drenched clothes.

Moment for Reflection

You see, it's not about what car you drive, how big your house is, or the amount on your paycheck. Honestly, think about what is left when all of that is taken away (or doesn't even exist). What are the little things in your day-to-day that can start putting a smile on your face instead of being a nuisance? Take a few minutes to list at least 10 of them now.

Little things (that could be GREAT things)

1. _____   6. _____
2. _____   7. _____
3. _____   8. _____
4. _____   9. _____
5. _____   10. _____

Jesus tells us in the book of Matthew not to store up treasures here on earth (Matthew 6:19–21, NLT). We can't take anything with us to heaven, and we can't prevent any of those things from being stolen or destroyed. So instead, cultivate what matters. Observe the little things that almost seem mundane but that can ultimately be so life-giving. Spend the extra few minutes talking to your co-worker about their weekend or playing blocks with your two-year-old. Sip the tea (read: coffee, if that is what your cup is filled with) with a thankful heart and wake up to admire the sunrise once in a while. Forgive that person who cut you off in traffic, for you never know what they are facing, and give that old friend a call to catch up.

6

Back to the States

Regresé a los Estados Unidos y a veces olvidé hablar Inglés. Todavía estaba pensando en Español y faltando mis amigos en Guatebuena.
I transitioned slowly back to English and often found myself slipping back into Spanish without even realizing it. For the benefit of those of you who aren't bilingual, I'll stick to English!

Ironically, the summer I returned home was undoubtedly the point of no return in my life. My previously decided future was now very much unknown. My dad had just remarried in May, my ex-boyfriend was now tearfully begging me to forgive him, my sister was treating every single person in her life like dirt, and I was about to leave in a week and a half for St. Thomas, where my mom would marry a Naval Senior Chief who had captured her heart. Despite the tearful pleas, I knew our breakup was for the best, and I planned to mend my broken heart on the sunny shores and in the salty sprays of the Caribbean.

The week away with family was just what I needed. Endless hours of pool volleyball brought joy to my heart, and the fresh mahi mahi and delicious strawberry daiquiris brought joy to my stomach. We spent a few days taking advantage of all that the resort had to offer, and I truly enjoyed catching up with my brother and sister after being away for half a year.

The calm breeze that carried a hint of saltiness into our room awoke us on the day of the wedding. My sister, mom, and I eagerly got dressed, did our hair and makeup, and headed outside to (illegally?) pick a few sprigs of local flowers for our bouquets. We rode in style in a couple of Rolls Royce's to a secluded beach for the ceremony. The intimate setting, underneath a double rainbow no less, was perfect as four of my mom and step-dad-to-be's friends, my grandma and grandpa, my soon-to-be step brother, my siblings, and I encircled my mom and step dad-to-be. A sweet ceremony came to a climax as the bride and groom kissed at the exact moment that a flock of parrots flew overhead (you can't make this stuff up!). Afterwards, several of us were baptized and re-dedicated our lives to Jesus in the bay—what a precious moment in a beautiful place.

As a group, we walked along the beach, laughing and taking pictures as we made everlasting memories. Our destination was a forty-five-foot sailboat where my mom and stepdad would spend their honeymoon. So, I guess it wasn't everyone's destination–just theirs. We said our goodbyes as they sailed off into the sunset (literally). The rest of us spent the next couple of days enjoying the beachy vibe for a little bit longer before we safely returned to the much less exciting, and a little less crystal blue, waters of Green Bay.

As I briefly mentioned, my sister was less than approachable over the next month and a half. I'll tell you in a sentence what it took all of us (including her) a few months to realize: she was pregnant. Her hormones said awful things to me, and before I knew they were the culprits, I was wishing I had left her in Guatemala.

Once everyone knew the cause of her mean streak, our hurt and frustration turned into support. Although she was young, we knew her only option was to raise the baby. I'm not going to go all "holier than thou" on you here, and heaven knows this is a divisive topic in our country, but I do have a few things to say. I want you to hear me clearly and know that all of this comes from a place of love. Love for the miracle of life that happens when an embryo is formed in a woman's womb. Jesus performed many miracles during his ministry, but in my opinion, no miracle is more astounding than the one that creates a tiny human. Abortion is murder. As hard as one tries to sugar coat it, you really can't make that reality easy to swallow. The points-of-view, arguments, and stances are endless, but just know that God values every single human that exists, because we are made in His image (Genesis 1:27) and we are His creation. That includes humans in the womb.

During this difficult time, I relied on Chris' friendship and long phone conversations to get me through the summer. Our platonic relationship was still platonic, but my feelings were starting to suggest otherwise. I was thoroughly convinced that having a crush on my best friend was a recipe for disaster, so I didn't say a word to anyone. He called me at the beginning of July and somewhat morosely discussed his breakup with his half-way-across-the-world girlfriend, and I dutifully offered my "best friend" condolences as I did a happy dance in my head. To be fair, their relationship was not benefiting either of them, and he wasn't being treated well. I was tired of watching him go through the motions, so I was celebrating his freedom from that (as well as his new-found availability to hang).

Come August, I had a case of cabin fever. I decided to take a three-week vacation. I headed to Madison to visit one of my best friends from high school, Ang. It was refreshing to catch up and spend some time in such a cool city. Sharing my feelings for Chris with her was also a relief and she suggested I share them with him. My fear of rejection led me to keeping them to myself–at least for a little while longer. Thanking her for such a fun two days, I continued my trek to Elmhurst to visit college friends I hadn't seen in a semester.

Our college was putting on an event locally, so my friend Nik and I joined Chris and headed there to meet up with some of our other friends. The night before, HB and I had a lengthy phone conversation about my emerging romantic feelings for Chris and he attempted to convince me to do the same thing Ang had suggested. At the event, HB pulled Chris into the other room and didn't return for several minutes. Suspiciously, we all carried on for the rest of the event as if nothing had happened.

Outback Steakhouse was on the menu for dinner, and you could cut the awkward tension with a steak knife. Our poor friends Tyla and Nik were witnesses to an avoidance game. Neither Chris nor I wanted to admit our feelings to each other, so we haphazardly talked about unimportant things while we tried to figure out this uncharted territory in our friendship. After the four of us got delicious frozen yogurt, Chris drove Nik and I to her house, as I had been staying there. The whole way home, Nik and I had been texting, as I silently worried about what to say or not to say.

When we arrived at her house, Nik quickly found an excuse to leave the car that conveniently didn't provide one for me. So, there we sat. In silence.

"Can I kiss you?"

Of course, inside I was melting from the sweetness, but also screaming at the importance of the next thirty seconds. I could not stand the idea that our friendship could be put into jeopardy if I said yes. So, I just didn't say anything.

long pause

"Amber, if you don't get out of this car, I am going to kiss you."

long pause (no exiting of the car)

He leaned over and gave me the sweetest, most tender kiss. It held so much emotion. I gave into the moment and kissed him back. I had just kissed my best friend. Could I finally start believing that he might actually like me back?

I texted Nik and told her I would be back later. I somehow found my voice again and desperately told Chris all of my feelings. How I was afraid and didn't want this to change our friendship. How I wasn't really ready to jump into being boyfriend/girlfriend since I had just left a five-year relationship. How I really liked him, and really liked that kiss. Surprisingly, he shared all of those feelings with me. We laughed about the irony of our current situation and agreed that we didn't need to rush into anything. After all, being friends was pretty great already. We spent the next day hanging out and swimming in his family's pool.

My professor picked me up from Chris' house and we took a road trip to Canada to see some of the Canadians who we had befriended on their school trip to Guatemala. It was NOT weird that I drove 500 miles with my professor. Thankfully, he had become kind of like an uncle to me during my time at Carthage College. He was my advisor, had helped me through some big career-altering decisions, and had helped plan and coordinate my semester abroad. Anyway, we spent the next few days with some awesome people in Toronto. He left to go spend a week with some family he had there, and I took a trip to Niagara Falls. What an amazing landform! The gushing power of those falls is incredible to witness—another place to add to your Google and travel lists!

After Canada, I ventured to Phoenix to enjoy desert hikes and ice cream cones with family I hadn't seen in awhile. While there, Chris and I chatted on the phone every day. He was waiting anxiously for me at O'Hare when I returned, and that night over dinner he cheesily (read: romantically) asked me to be his girlfriend. Things had progressed quickly since that day three weeks earlier when we had claimed we didn't want to rush into a relationship. Nevertheless, we were head over heels and things just felt right. Dating Chris was everything I wanted in a relationship, and our friends were quick to point out that they "knew it all along."

Things felt right, until they didn't. Nothing to do with Chris, of course. He and I were great. Rather, my migraines hadn't gone away, and I was to the point where I wanted to try some prophylactic medication instead of my twice-daily diet of Excedrin Migraine. My doctor suggested Topamax (topiramate) which is an anti-seizure medication that is also often used to prevent migraines. I had tried Imitrex and other migraine pain meds, with little success and many adverse effects, but I figured I'd give this one a try. As many do, this drug supposedly takes a few weeks to start taking effect, so I dutifully took it for a couple of months that fall.

As I was weaning myself onto the medication, I encountered life-altering brain fog and bouts of dizziness. One morning, I woke up on the shower floor after I had passed out and hit my head on the wall, seemingly from low blood pressure. Chris and my roommate spent the next two days monitoring my concussion symptoms. I was thankful the fall didn't cause worse injuries!

In terms of college and graduation, I had plans to attend physical therapy school upon leaving Carthage, so I took the GRE. Despite having never finished less than the 98th percentile on a standardized test, I was struggling to maintain focus during the exam. My mind was cloudy and I finished with only a few minutes to spare. It was then that I realized how much Topamax had influenced my future. I did not do well enough on the GRE to get accepted to a physical therapy school. My hopes were dashed. As a daughter of a nurse and a respiratory therapist, my plans had long included medical school. I had interned a few summers in physical therapy offices both inpatient and outpatient, and when my plans to become a doctor didn't seem easily attainable, I needed to make a quick course correction.

Thankfully, since I was planning to double major in Spanish and Chemistry, it was easy to drop the Chemistry major to a minor and pursue a few more advanced Spanish Literature courses. (Disclaimer: When this was happening, I was confused and frustrated, but looking back on this now, this was such a God-thing. With what's to come, a career in the medical field would've been next to impossible.) My new plan included getting hired as a teacher (with a bachelor's degree in Spanish) and teaching high school Spanish as I worked toward my teaching certificate in graduate school. Suddenly very thankful for the teaching I had done in Guatemala, I interviewed at a small charter school in Kenosha.

Despite not having a teaching degree, the interview left me feeling hopeful. The staff members I conversed with were friendly and had a passion for educating that I was beginning to feel myself! The principal said I would hear from him by the end of the week. Heading into the sunshine, I made my way to the park across the street that lined the Lake Michigan harbor. I remember thanking God for how He had guided my steps thus far and prayed I would get the chance to teach at such an awesome school. That is precisely why the devastation hit hard that afternoon when Will called to share that he offered the job to a more experienced teacher. God must've had a different plan, and I was determined to figure out what it was.

The next day, as I sat in front of my computer filling out an application, I saw Will's name on my phone. Wondering why he was calling after our most recent talk, I answered hesitantly.

"Amber, I know our conversation yesterday was hard, but I am calling to offer you the position and hoping you'll accept."

Rather shocked, I graciously accepted. Over the next few minutes, he explained that the board had required him to offer the position to the more qualified teacher, but since that guy had accepted another job in Arizona, he was excited to work with me. I headed back to the same spot I had prayed in the day before and thanked God for His faithfulness. His path for us is not always the easy one or the one we would choose, but I am grateful that He is in control and not me. The school lived up to my expectations as a fabulous place that believed in a hands-on approach to learning (no textbooks here, folks!), was filled with motivated educators and (mostly) excited students, and provided an opportunity for me to plan and create my own curricula for five different levels of Spanish.

Even with the inordinate amount of work, I loved every second of it! My love for the Spanish language came shining through in my creative, exciting lessons (that last part could've been written by my students—I'm sure of it!). I structured my courses differently than the language courses I had taken in school, speaking only in Spanish (even with my freshmen) and helping students utilize and participate within all four language domains every day: listening, speaking, reading, and writing. By the end of the first semester of my level 202 class, I remember them thanking me for the challenge and claiming they'd learned more that semester than all of their other Spanish classes combined. Secret is: they were doing a lot of the learning on their own.

Ya know, that's the key to learning a language. You have to use it purposefully, like, for real reasons. Go to a restaurant and try ordering in your second language. How would you navigate a new city without using your first language? Need to ask where the *pepinos* are in a Spanish market? Or maybe you just need to talk to the exchange student—start with hello. When you make language learning (or any learning, really) purposeful and practical, it helps your brain retain the information.

Do not be
yoked
with unbelievers
for what do
righteousness
& wickedness
have in common?
Or what fellowship
can light have
with darkness

2 Corinthians 6:14
NIV

The Right Relationships

Some of the relationships we invest in are chosen for us: i.e. parent-child relationship, sibling relationship, teacher-student relationship, etc. Other relationships we invest in are chosen by us. Both are important. Both take work. But it's the latter that takes wisdom. You know when you are in a relationship, friendly or romantic, that just doesn't feel right. You're putting in all the effort and not getting much in return, or your partner/friend seems clingy and you're not motivated to spend time with them. Or maybe you have a friend who always tries to convince you to do something you know is a poor choice. If those things are happening, get outta dodge! No, seriously, run the other direction.

Moment for Reflection

Take some time to reflect on the role you have in your relationships. Are you the best friend you can be? Do you purpose to serve others? How often do you expect to get things out of those relationships rather than pour into them? Write two ways in which you can be intentional about strengthening your relationships this week.

_____

_____

_____

_____

_____

_____

_____

_____

_____

_____

7

Brain Surgery

Seven blissful months had passed. Chris and I were celebrating with a delicious dinner. Remember, though, when I said "things felt right, until they didn't"? My post-dinner experience wasn't pleasant, and as my neck pain intensified, we headed to the hospital. Let me be clear: getting me to the hospital is like getting a tooth pulled. It's not going to happen until there's no other option. So, this certainly wasn't normal neck pain (whatever that is). Once at the ER, the intense pressure rush of getting out of the car was almost too much to tolerate. Chris gently carried me out and set me, half-laying, in the wheelchair. The doctor, after taking one look at me and after hearing my symptoms, wanted to do a lumbar puncture to check my white blood cell count, suspecting meningitis or some other infection.

Now, if you don't know, just doing a lumbar puncture (spinal tap) runs its own risks, therefore, it's important that the situation warrants one. Sticking a foreign object (sterile needle in this case) into your spinal fluid could cause a spinal headache (already had a migraine, so that risk was irrelevant) or even potentially cause an infection on its own. Not only are there the "what-ifs," but there are also the realities and the "for-sures." It's extremely painful as you are in a fetal position on the table and the procedure usually lasts just under an hour. Anyway, the need for information outweighed the risks, so the doctor did the procedure and I laid on my back for hours afterwards. This is supposed to prevent a spinal headache (remember, I already had a migraine), and help the healing. The results were staggering, as my white blood cell count was extremely high. Clearly, there was something wrong, and my body was sending all the soldiers to the front line! My amazement caused by the effectiveness and efficiency of the human body will never cease. We are designed so intricately to survive in a world that constantly tries to bring us down.

I was promptly admitted, diagnosed with meningitis, and then began the scavenger hunt. Since bacteria didn't grow in the sample of spinal fluid they took, they assumed it was viral meningitis. The medical team really had no idea what could have caused it and what was making me so sick, even after the heavy dose of antibiotics, so they continued to search. It kinda felt like I was the board in the game Operation. I mean, they poked and prodded me everywhere and asked me some of the silliest questions. The buzzer was continually sounding off though, because they certainly had not been able to narrow down anything.

As we came to day four, after determining I didn't have HIV or an STD, the doctors wanted to do a bone marrow biopsy. This type of immune response could be triggered by cancer, they thought, so let's drill into her bone and take out some bone marrow. Maybe you missed that last part–they *drilled* into my bone. Not with an actual drill. No, it was much worse than that. They used a handheld one so that I could feel every turn of the bit as it dug into my thick hip bone (later, I will realize how thankful I should have been that my hip bone was, indeed, thick). On top of all of that, we now had a week to wonder if we would have to face a cancer diagnosis.

The lumbar puncture and bone marrow biopsy weren't the only fun I got to have that week! The next day, day five of my stay, my morning "up and at'em" from the nurse was a purplish-gray slush mix that I had to drink before my four-hour brain and cervical MRI with contrast. MRIs weren't a new thing for me, as I had already spent hours in that tube filled with little hammering gnomes (if you've been in one, you know what I mean!). Spending four *consecutive* hours inside was new though. So, thankfully, because I still had a migraine, they were planning to give me a relaxant to help me get through it. After I downed my slurry sip by sip, I boastfully told the nurse I had finished with three minutes to spare on my time limit. She handed me another cupful. Gah, as if one wasn't enough! I managed to finish that one before the transport tech came to cart me to the basement.

The experience was far from relaxing, as this tube not only had the hammering gnomes, but also tiny eskimos sticking ice picks into the back of my head due to the fact that my mother had french braided my hair that morning causing me to lay on a braid for the duration of the MRI. I no longer braid my hair straight down the back of my head, just in case I ever need to pop into one of those machines with short notice!

Liquid in places it shouldn't be is almost always a problem, especially in your body. Apparently it looked like I had liquid or swelling behind my ear, so the doctor investigated further. What he found provided an interesting diagnosis, which seemed to explain some of my lifelong symptoms: Chiari malformation. *Eight* out of 1,000 people have this disease, so it's classified as *rare*. As the doctor explained that my brainstem hung below my skull about five cm, my family quickly employed humor as a coping mechanism and joked that they always knew my brain was too big for my head. They laughed that I had read too many books and that I had somehow caused this with my hours of studying. The truth was that no one had done anything to cause it, and it was simply how God had formed me. Now, I do not believe God makes mistakes, so, even though my anatomy wasn't how it was "supposed" to be physically, I knew that there had to be a reason I had been created that way.

It was curious that they had never seen the Chiari malformation on any of the previous MRIs, but I was thankful they noticed it this time! It finally proposed an explanation for my migraines. Often people with Chiari malformation suffer from migraines because the skull can put pressure on the spinal cord. That doesn't sound very comfy, does it? As I heard the list of other potential symptoms, I thanked God that I only suffered from migraines! I hadn't yet incurred nerve pain, frequent vomiting, dizziness, or loss of mobility. As you can imagine, since your spinal cord does a lot for you, it is not good when it is being pressed on.

The doctor finished explaining the options I had: have surgery or don't. Surgery obviously always comes with a long list of "potentials," especially when they are operating so near to the brain. This surgery in particular, a suboccipital decompression, involves going in at the base of the skull and essentially scraping the bone there to make more room for the cerebellum and spinal cord (a procedure called a craniectomy). When necessary, the surgeon may also cut the dura (the layer of tissue surrounding the brain) and remove the cerebellar tonsils in a procedure called electrocautery ("Office of Neuroscience"). The tonsils have no known function, and can be removed without causing any neurological effects.

Not having surgery, on the other hand, can lead to a higher severity of symptoms and an increased risk of paralysis. Like I mentioned, at this point, it seemed my only symptom of the malformation was the migraines. I do not want to downplay them, because they came daily, were fairly terrible, and often led to me not participating in normal activities, but I am grateful that I wasn't experiencing any of the other serious symptoms.

We opted for surgery, to avoid the worsening of symptoms, and had it scheduled for a few weeks later. I quickly went from never having broken a bone or having any type of surgery, to contacting a brain surgeon to operate on me. Big jump. After being discharged from the hospital, I initiated the dreaded FMLA paperwork to prepare for a leave of absence from my teaching job. After missing a week and a half of school, my students were thankful I was back. I regretfully explained that I would have to leave them again at the beginning of April and should return before the end of the year. The supportive responses I received from staff, students, family, and friends was overwhelming. I was thankful for the notes, cards, and of course, the prayers being said on my behalf.

The week after I left the hospital, I made my way to the oncologist's office with Chris, my mom, my stepdad, and my grandparents, to hear the results of the bone marrow biopsy. I was thankful to have family by my side during this trying time. My *thoughts* since leaving the hospital teetered between faith and fear. What would a cancer diagnosis mean? God knows. Chemo? Good thing God has allowed humans this treatment option. Losing my hair? A radical lifestyle change? My *prayers* since leaving the hospital mostly consisted of "Thy will be done." I knew that whatever the results were, God is faithful and He knows my future. If the doctor was going to say the dreaded c word, it would be no surprise to Him.

As I sat there with tears in my eyes, I honestly couldn't believe the words I was hearing from her mouth. There was no cancer! My white cell count was extremely high, most likely due to meningitis and nothing else. The tears were an outward sign of the inward joy I was experiencing. Relief doesn't really sum up what I was feeling, but it was so much more than that. Joy, gratitude, shock, happiness, strength, and resiliency were all unraveling from the knot that had tightened in my gut throughout the last week. My family exuded many of those emotions as well as we all hugged, high fived, and cried. I remember my mom pulling me close and whispering, "God is good."

I was thankful for modern medicine that could rule out nastiness and grateful that God had heard some prayers. We considered a second opinion (because we all know that humans, and tests, make mistakes) but decided against it. If cancer lurked somewhere in my body, it would manifest its nasty head and be found eventually.

Now that I avoided that hurdle, I turned to a question I didn't really know how to answer: how do you prepare for brain surgery? I listened to the surgeon's preparatory statements and acknowledged the questions and answers I heard from both him, my mom, and my boyfriend (Can we just talk about that for a second—Chris and I had been friends for awhile, but had only been dating for a little more than half a year, and yet here he was by my side as I faced a week-long hospital stay, a possible cancer diagnosis, and brain surgery—boyfriend of the year!).

To be honest, I didn't google much more about the surgery or Chiari than the definitions. The information I had gleaned from conversations over the last month was enough for me. After Dr. Wave nonchalantly told me that my roller coaster-riding days should have never existed, he elaborated on the extreme danger I had been in. The pressure my skull had been putting on my brain stem, combined with the change in pressure I experienced while riding on a roller coaster, could have easily resulted much more tragically than any of my joyful rides ever did. My prayer going in was simply that I would come out myself (no neurological differences) and that I would experience relief from migraines. I also thanked God for what I had avoided as a child.

For me, learning *enough* about my disease to understand the process was *enough*. I don't obsessively research it, and I think that's okay.

The surgeon himself was pretty chill, especially for a guy who literally holds people's lives in his hands with each operation. One wrong move has the potential to cause paralysis or worse. I imagine it's not a profession for the high strung, and since he's the only brain surgeon I've ever talked to, he confirms my hypothesis. Whether or not that is true of others, I was thankful for his cool composure and natural ability to make us feel very at ease. Ultimately, knowing that God had it all in His hands, there was no fear and really not even any anxiousness. The army of prayer warriors that I had on my side, whispering prayers to heaven for my safety and full recovery, supernaturally supported me through what was next.

The day had come. The day I would become a zipperhead (that's what they call people who have this surgery because the scar literally looks like a zipper up the back of your neck and head). I knew that before operating, the nurse would shave several inches of my hair from the nape of my neck to the crown of my head. I wasn't excited about it, but I quickly reminded myself that it would be hardly noticeable, much unlike losing your hair due to chemotherapy. Grateful, I said a prayer of thanksgiving that morning, that I would get to keep most of my hair. It may seem like a vain prayer, and it probably is, but when you are faced with big scary things like brain surgery, you have to celebrate the little things. For only God knew the results of the surgery to come. As I mentioned earlier, I was trusting Him for a successful surgery and a full recovery.

Some of my family came to spend those last moments with me before I was wheeled away. My one-year-old niece provided some comic relief and adorableness as she tottered around the hospital bed with that goofy grin never leaving her face. My mom brought her steadfast faith, and my sister and brother brought their upbeat positivity. Chris was also there with his gorgeous (somewhat tense) smile. We prayed together and they lifted me into the hands of the surgeon and our heavenly father. After the administering of the anesthesia, I don't remember anything until I woke up four and a half hours later in the ICU having to lay flat in my intense pain.

Surgery went well, although they did have to cover my dura with an artificial dura patch because it was so thin. A little discomforting was the fact that my spine and skull both had several holes in them and looked similar to swiss cheese. At that time, the surgeon didn't know what to tell us about this and explained that he would send the bone sample to a lab in New York and wait to hear about a diagnosis. Until then, we would wait and wonder. In typical fashion, I was presenting as a medical conundrum.

More unknown.

More waiting.

More praying.

Recovery

My most vivid memory from that first night in the ICU is filled with excruciating pain. It was pitch black and I was surrounded by strangers in masks. I kept trying to tell them about the pain, but it didn't seem to matter to them. My neck had just been cut open, and my head felt like an anvil was smashing it to the bed, but they had a job to do. One of the nurses told me they were going to move me from the bed to the table. I was screaming on the inside; I hardly knew who or where I was, but I knew they weren't asking my opinion. Then I felt the pain grip me so severely that I couldn't help but cry out as they lifted the corners of the sheet and dropped me (whether or not they were gentle, it felt like a drop) onto the table for the CT scan. The memory goes black.

Morning always seems a little brighter, even if you are relying on your morphine drip to keep you from crying. I floated in and out of sleep for the next day or two, but I can remember that my mom and Chris were there watching movies and talking to me when I opened my eyes. The third morning post-surgery was when I almost regretted them keeping most of my hair. I don't know *what* happened on the operating table, but my hair was a literal rat's nest, and my mom was struggling to get a comb through it millimeter by millimeter. On top of the snarly hair, any movement of my head brought waves of pain. One of the nurses commented that they should have told me to braid it before surgery. Too. Late. I think I pleaded for my mom to just shave it, but thankfully she didn't listen to my painkiller-induced foggy pleas. Instead, she spent hours gently combing through what hair I had left. She eventually got it into a ponytail and showed me the back of my head for the first time since surgery.

If you have long hair, wear it in french-braided pigtails for surgery.

"That is not me." I remember thinking over and over as I looked into the mirror and saw the reflection of red, stitched flesh. I think this moment is as close to an out-of-body experience as I've had. It seemed to my brain that my eyes were playing a trick on me. The moment was very surreal as I heard my mom and Chris reassure me that the reflection was mine and that it would heal beautifully and be less than noticeable. My mom even tried comforting me with the knowledge that my long hair would cover it anyway. Those things all turned out to be true. My hair did cover my scar, it healed well, and was hardly noticeable, but to this day I struggle to look at pictures from that time and acknowledge that it is actually me.

The only other memory I have from my recovery room is filled with pain, but also fear. Again, it is dark. Night time. I awake on some sort of spaceship, or at least in a technologically advanced medical rehabilitation center. Lights are blinking everywhere, and I am struggling to lift my head to look beyond the blinking lights, but I can't. I'm stuck in bed. Through the door walks a very large man. He mumbles something to me that I fail to comprehend properly, and suddenly my brain tells me he is here to run an experiment on me. I sleepily struggle to deny him the chance, but again, am unable to move. He takes my vitals and leaves the room. Drugs do weird things to your brain, even when they are being used in a positive way to help you through healing and pain. Once I called out to Chris, he assured me that the man was taking good care of me as my nurse, and we were most definitely not on a spaceship. I was thankful, but he may have been a little bummed out that we weren't actually in fact flying through space and time.

Actually, one more quick one (and it was, indeed, much quicker than I expected). I had a lumbar drain inserted during surgery to avoid pooling of my CSF (cerebrospinal fluid). Of course, while it was in, I couldn't feel it, but the moment came when it was time to remove it. We were grateful it had served its purpose and there hadn't been any complications. The nurse assured me it would be painless and be over before I knew it. As I leaned forward in bed, I felt the small plastic tube exit my body in a very noodly fashion. It really is the only way I can describe that fantastical experience. It reminded me of sucking a spaghetti noodle through my lips on pasta night. No pain. Just weird.

Albeit much faster than our original expectations, my recovery seemed long and drawn out. I was home after less than a week in the hospital and was moving around fairly easily on my own. Of course, I couldn't lift anything heavier than a gallon of milk or shower on my own, so I was grateful for the help from my mom, Chris, my roommate, and friends who visited. Suddenly losing the ability to care for yourself in most senses of the word is a difficult thing. The pain remained, but I purposed to stretch and move my neck and head to encourage healing. I could've easily come out of that surgery being upset at how my life had suddenly changed, but I chose to work hard through recovery, stay positive, and keep things as normal as possible. After all, I was rejoicing and praising God for bringing me safely through surgery—what did I have to be upset about?

The next several months were filled with lots of medication, doctor visits, and the game Rummikub (thanks, EL). Six short weeks post-op, I actually did go back to work to close out the school year. Thankfully, my substitute had done a fantastic job, and I was left only with the difficult task of saying goodbye to my students for the summer.

I knew you before I formed you in your Mother's Womb.

Jeremiah 1:5 NLT

God Doesn't Make Mistakes

We have talked a little bit about how my eyes are different sizes. Not only that, but they are bigger than most people's eyes. Not really in the "cute like a cartoon princess," way either, but more like "scary and weird like a monster." Maybe I am being a little dramatic, but I've always felt embarrassed and self-conscious about the size of them. Many people have made comments over the years (most were very well-intentioned), which hasn't helped to ease my heightened awareness of the oddity.

Despite all of that, a few years ago, I realized that God created me, in His image, and my eyes are exactly how He planned for them to be. Instead of letting the awkwardness take over and squinting all the time (which I still do on occasion), I thank Him that I can see His beauty all around me. I know each one of us is unique and special in physical attributes as well as personality and spirit. It's a blessing that we are not all the same and that we have identifying features. I am thankful for my eyes and try not to worry about them so much.

Similarly, I know that my physical deformities were created intentionally. For one thing, they have allowed me to share this story with you about how God is perfect and His plan is without flaw. For another thing, my faith has been strengthened because of the medical trials I have walked (and laid, and cried, and slept) through.

Praise God for the pieces of yourself that you don't like to show the world. Thank Him for the belly fat leftover from growing your precious babies, or your too-big nose that allows you to smell flowers and chocolate chip cookies, or your chronic disease that helps you walk by faith and draws you closer to Him.

Moment for Reflection

Do you have a physical attribute that you don't love about yourself? Take a moment to thank God that He created you with it! You are beautiful and loved by your Creator.

_____

_____

_____

_____

_____

_____

_____

_____

_____

_____

_____

8

A Dr. Seuss Diagnosis

The phone rang. In the parking lot of Home Depot, Chris and I listened intently as Dr. Wave explained a report that compared my bones to something out of a Dr. Seuss book. If you've never been told that (which I doubt you have, because how ridiculous is that?!), you may not know what a fair reaction to that is. An abrupt laugh sounded from my mouth, as my brain tried to make sense of what my ears were hearing. Is that really what he just said? Dr. Seuss is no medical doctor, yet he has somehow made his way into this extremely scientific conversation about a serious, rare, life-altering diagnosis. Somehow I made my way through the rest of the conversation as he explained I had a disease called lymphangiomatosis. He told me what little they knew about it, which was basically the name, that it affected my lymph system, and that only about 8 in 10,000 people have it. If you're into decimals, that is .0008 or .08% of people.

Finally, the migraines, knee pain, and swelling had a name. We could research a name. We could pray for healing from it. We could find others with it and a doctor who specialized in it. So, that's what we did.

The day I met Dr. K was the day I had longed for my entire life. After the friendly greetings, he simply asked me to tell him everything I could about my health history; even if it seemed irrelevant or overlooked in the past, I should share. One by one,

I named the little pieces of my story that suddenly had meaning. After each revelation, this person sitting in front of me confirmed that these issues, including the eye size that had led to my awkward nickname in elementary school and the three-and-a-half-inch cyst they found when I had my wisdom teeth removed the year before, were each a result or symptom of my newly-named disease. The relief and validation flooded over me. The moment that many people with rare diseases dream of, was finally happening for me. I had a doctor, listening to me, confirming that: I wasn't mistaken, it was not all in my head, and there certainly was a reason for the crackling in my knee, the daily migraines, the chronic pain, and the malformation they had just corrected with surgery.

I want to be clear that years of feeling unheard, ignored, and misdiagnosed can lead to a lot of frustration. I had pretty much lost faith in doctors and medicine in general. My trust in medical experts had all but vanished (excluding my parents of course, who were both in the medical field), consequent to past experiences, but each confirmation from Dr. K knocked down a brick from that wall I had built. Lymphangiomatosis provided an explanation, or at least a supposed one, for almost every question mark we had from the past twenty three years. My mom, Chris, and I spent most of that conversation smiling, nodding, and cheering as each brick fell.

The respect and gratefulness I now had for this man was astounding. In him, I had an advocate who could guide me through the unknown. He explained a little bit more about the disease. The other names it had (which would also be googled extensively by my curious mother) were Gorham's Disease or "disappearing bone disease," because at its simplest sense, it is pockets of lymph fluid that exist outside of the normal lymphatic system that eat away at bone or soft tissue. Let that one sink in for a minute. My lymph system was malformed (in utero), and extra lymph was rogue in several parts of my body, including my spine and my skull. It was essentially eating holes in those very integral bones. Through my confirmation, and validation, the real sense of how serious this disease was dampered our spirits a bit.

Although it is often diagnosed in childhood, mine had gone undiagnosed until my early 20's. The doctor continued to explain that there were few patients they knew with the disease and that my story would most likely be met with fascination by all who heard it. Afterall, he was an "expert" on this rare vascular anomaly after having cared for a whopping eight children. Since he was a pediatric oncologist, I was his oldest patient at twenty three, so I presented an even more peculiar case. Thankfully, though, I was much better off than many with this awful disease. Almost all of the children Dr. K had worked with, had legs so swollen they couldn't walk. Some had so much lymph in their swollen arms that they couldn't ride a bike or play sports. I said a silent prayer of thanksgiving right then and there that despite some abnormal symptoms, and years filled with migraine headaches, I had played and enjoyed life as a relatively uninhibited child.

It was during that same meeting that we also learned how lymphangiomatosis and Chiari malformation are related. Dr. K had asked about my history of contact sports and roller coasters. He explained the risk of each while living with Chiari and revealed that many children who are diagnosed with the malformation wear helmets to protect the brain and spinal cord from any possible damage. You've heard it: hindsight is 20/20. The roller coaster-loving, three-sport athlete life was probably not the best choice looking back, but I was thankful I hadn't known about the risk beforehand. Here's another one: sometimes ignorance really *is* bliss.

When you read the name of the disease a few paragraphs ago, you may have thought "lymphoma." Similarly to lymphoma, this disease affects the lymph system and is an autoimmune disorder that suppresses the immune system, but thankfully, it is not cancer. Since honesty is what this whole story has been about, I will hesitantly admit that I've often wished my diagnosis was fundraised for, fought against, and understood by society like cancer is. That is not to take the seriousness away from cancer, but just to add credence and gravity to lymphangiomatosis. The prognosis is often not as short as someone diagnosed with, say, stage four liver cancer, but it is incurable, treated with cancer drugs, can be very disruptive to everyday life, and can lead to death. So, there are definitely similarities.

Since my symptoms were fairly regulated by over-the-counter pain medication, we decided against pursuing treatment. The proposed treatment would have been an immunosuppressant drug called sirolimus, which aims to slow the growth of the extracurricular lymph, but has also been used to treat cancer and to encourage successful organ transplants. The long list of side effects was not worth it, so we erred on the side of caution.

I found myself in the ER a few times that summer and fall with extreme neck pain. They gave me a few shots of Toradol and sent me (hours later) on my merry way. Chris and I enjoyed long summer days geocaching and swimming in the pool as our relationship was getting more serious with each found cache (if you don't know what on earth that means, go to geocaching.com–you're welcome).

August (four months post-op) brought another new experience: a positron emission tomography, or PET, scan. Dr. K wanted to see to what extent the lymphangiomatosis was affecting my organs and other soft tissue, and it would also double as a "double check" for the whole cancer thing. This scan is often done to detect and locate cancer or other diseases by introducing radioactive tracers into the body that then get absorbed by certain organs or tissues (Krans and Adcox). Diseased areas will collect more of the radioactive tracers and show brightly on the imaging.

The results garnered no new information, which meant no cancer and no soft tissue lymph involvement—Praise the Lord!

With the good news, and a (mostly) healed neck, I was welcomed back to my classroom(s). Any traveling teachers out there? Here is your shout out! I know you don't hear it often, or even at all, so soak it in. You. Are. Awesome! As a traveling teacher, I taught in several different classrooms in the school building throughout the day. I had to carry all of my supplies with me to each location. It is no easy task, as you can imagine. I had six different preps (meaning I planned for six levels of Spanish every two days), in a school where textbooks were considered mundane and unnecessary. Therefore, I spent many hours holed up in my stuffy office above the gym (literally as far away from my classrooms as physically possible) planning exhilarating lessons for somewhat unenthusiastic high schoolers who varied between apathetic and pretentious. I'm making it sound terrible without meaning to. I loved that job, and I loved those kids. The bouncing between classrooms and three–five hours a day I spent preparing were characteristics of the job I could've easily done without.

That semester, Chris and I were still doing the long distance thing. Wednesday night was date night. When we could, we each drove the forty five minutes to our rendezvous point for dinner: Gurnee Mills Mall. We were young and in love, and obviously excited to see each other during the week, so of course we headed there right after work. This meant we often ate surrounded by old folks and even got "early bird" specials on occasion. I believe our relationship was tested and strengthened during this time (I mean, if it hadn't been solidified enough by enduring brain surgery together), and I am grateful for it. Long distance is definitely hard, but it allows you space and time to really learn about each other and talk about important things like the latest movie, the Cubs' record, how we felt about having kids, and getting married. Like I said, after all we had endured together, and after being friends for years, we were serious about our relationship from the beginning.

The months flew by with the busyness of it all, and I found myself sitting at my desk in my once stuffy, now drafty, office. It was the end of finals week, so I was inevitably grading an exorbitant amount of travel brochures, restaurant menus, and conversation videos. I remember one of the videos was an episode of Dora the Explorer that one of the groups in my 102 class had done, and I was beaming with pride when the phone rang. I smiled as I answered the phone and heard Chris' chipper voice on the other line. He asked if I wanted to take a walk at the beach in a couple hours. Of course, I normally jumped at the idea of a romantic walk on the shoreline, but in December? Despite my lack of enthusiasm for freezing, I agreed to meet.

Giving him time to arrive from his home over an hour away, I met him at the parking lot of our favorite beach (the one where we first said "I love you" over a year and a half earlier). He quietly took my hand as we walked toward the entrance to the beach. At this point, I knew something was up, whereas I had only been suspicious after the phone call. He was silent for the entire one-hundred-yard walk, and once we hit the sand, he turned to look at me. Now, it was December, in southern Wisconsin, so I could undoubtedly feel the wind slapping my face, but that's not the part I remember. He took a small gift box out of his pocket and said he wanted to give me one of my Christmas gifts early. I had goosebumps (not only from the wind) as I opened the box and realized it was empty. He sheepishly started looking around on the ground as if something must've fallen out and then gracefully landed on one knee. There was no elaborate speech (for which I tease him to this day), but nevertheless, he asked me to marry him. The love (and relief) in his eyes was abundant as I immediately agreed and we hugged and kissed as the sand blew in our hair.

We rehashed the sweet, special moment at one of our favorite tapas restaurants in the next town. Over sangria and paella (love me some Spanish food and drink), we thanked God for the tough stuff He had already brought us through, which had strengthened our love, and reminisced about the laughable silliness we continued to enjoy day in and day out. Those little moments (and the big ones) were now going to become part of our forever, and we couldn't have been more excited!

If he stays by your side through brain surgery—
marry him! Haha

---

trust in the
Lord
with
ALL YOUR
♡

LEAN NOT
on your own
understanding
in all your
ways
acknowledge
HIM

Proverbs 3 5-6a
ESV

Life Changes

So, if you're keeping track: I started 2011 having brain surgery for a rare condition, shortly after getting diagnosed with an even more rare disease, and ended it getting engaged to the love of my life. Talk about a roller coaster of a big year!

God knows the future.

He gives it to us one step at a time.

In amounts we can handle.

Our human desire is to know each and every step, though. I think most of us, if offered the chance to see our future, would jump at it!

Thankfully, God knows better, and He doesn't even give us that chance.

Despite the frustration, pain, misdiagnoses, lack of medical empathy, and confusion, I am thankful that I wasn't diagnosed as a child. Graciously, God allowed me to have a relatively normal childhood. Had I known that my skull was putting pressure on my brain stem for twenty two years and any sudden trauma to the area could have paralyzed me or even led to instant death, my childhood would've been very different. I never would have risked the twirly rides at our favorite local amusement park or even the roller coasters at Six Flags (which I loved—once I was tall enough to ride them—in high school). I'm not sure that I would've played softball, or at least not as "all-out" as I did. My friends may have treated me cautiously and I'm sure I would've been ostracized or called names by others who knew that something was "weird" about me.

What I'm trying to say is that oftentimes (always), God keeping the future from us until His timing is right, is better than Him telling us when we want to know.

That's the other thing: He prepares us for what He is going to ask us to face. By the time I was diagnosed and underwent brain surgery, my faith was unwavering, and I had an extremely caring boyfriend by my side, as well as a supportive prayer army. The medical community knew very little about my disease at my diagnosis, so, any sooner, and I would've been even more of a guinea pig with symptom identification and treatment options.

Moment for Reflection

Can you think of a time or event in your life during which you realized you were well-prepared for it at that moment, but would've struggled if it had come even a moment sooner?

Write about that time now. Thank God for His provision, preparation, and perfect timing.

_____

_____

_____

_____

_____

_____

_____

_____

_____

_____

_____

_____

_____

_____

_____

_____

_____

_____

9

Marital Bliss

"Do you, Amber, promise to ... cherish ...?

"I do.

Wow, that was quick! I skipped over the nine months of wedding planning, because that was mostly filled with details that are probably only interesting to me (and maybe a handful of the rest of y'all). Our wedding day was beautiful, emotional, and love-filled, as we promised forever and danced the night away with three hundred of our closest family members and friends, and my awesome new sister and wonderful in-laws! Simply the best!

Next, we were off to jungle paradise for a week as newlyweds. Unfortunately, I had chosen my footwear poorly the night before and was paying for it as I could barely step on the ground the next morning. That's one thing I was realizing: this disease didn't take kindly to repetitive motion and really didn't like when I didn't cushion my body appropriately. My feet throbbed and I had to routinely be sure to stand up throughout the plane ride to Belize to stretch my legs.

As we stepped off the plane, the Belizean heat was stifling. The one room airport had no air conditioning and did little to relieve the heat. The beads of perspiration came quicker as we realized that my bag had been lost and there was little we could do about it. I was now in a foreign country with the clothes on my back and two pain pills, which would barely last through the night. I whispered a prayer as we exited the now-empty building.

The sign he was holding read "Mkall." A short, gruff looking man with a holey cowboy hat stood next to a pickup truck that looked a bit miniature. Since we were the only ones walking toward the lot, and he was the only one in it, we didn't have much of a choice but to throw Chris' bag (because mine was nowhere to be found) in the back and cram ourselves into the bench seat behind him. Choosing not to dwell on the dire situation I was in, I chatted away with our driver who happened to be very willing to share about the countryside he had spent his life in. I would say he was going well above the speed limit, but since there were no signs, I couldn't even tell you if that was true. The speedometer was broken, but as we flew past oncoming cars at what felt like at least 110 mph, they hardly seemed to flinch on the barely-more-than-one-lane road.

"This is how we drive here. Everyone does it." claimed our driver matter-of-factly.

I was relatively calm about it, as we had passed at least a dozen cars without dying. Unbeknownst to me, my newly-deemed life partner was daydreaming (nightmaring) about us dying in a head-on collision or being driven deep into the jungle to be left for dead. Chris didn't say a word for the entire fifty-five minute ride to the resort, that was indeed, deep in the jungle. Since we had spent so much time trying to figure out where my bag was, it was two hours later than we were scheduled to arrive. Belmont stopped the car amongst the trees. At least, that's where I assumed we were. There were no lights to be seen. Actually, there was nothing to be seen as the blackness of the jungle night surrounded us. Soon after the engine died, we saw bobbing beams of light to our right. Chris grabbed my hand as if his life depended on it. We exited the car and followed the men with the bouncy flashlights into the trees.

After what must've been no longer than a minute (but what

felt more like a lifetime) a beautiful aquamarine pool lit by tiki torches came into view. Further in the distance, the dinner patio was illuminated by the same glow of more torches and I felt Chris' grip loosen. We had arrived at our destination and were not being led to an untimely ending. Later, I would hear just how anxious Chris had been the entire time. I must start being more aware of what he's feeling, I thought, as I listened to him discuss how relieved he was that we had made it to our treehouse oasis.

The next morning, we met a one-with-the-earth couple from California. She was petite like me, had her hair tied up in a bandana, and spoke as if she lived on a surfboard. His dreadlocks and board shorts told a similar story. They were easy to talk to, and after the "Where are you froms?" and the "How long have you been married?," we shared our plight of my missing bag. Since we were about the same size, she generously offered me a bathing suit so I could at least enjoy the pool as we waited for my bag to hopefully show up. Without my hiking shoes, or anything other than my comfy travel clothes, we weren't planning on going on any excursions any time soon. I was grateful for her kindness, and we spent the next day and a half lounging by the pool, exploring the orchid greenhouses (that housed over 240 species), and walking the mostly-dry riverbed.

Our trip package included two jungle excursions, and I was doing my best to convince Chris that since we had survived our trip inland with a racecar driver, we could repel down a mountain once my stuff showed up. He raised the stakes by agreeing to that only if I would snorkel with him once we got to the beach three days later. I was terrified to say yes because of my petrifying fear of swimming with fish and/or any other creepy sea creature, but I really wanted to see his face as we repelled down the mountain, so it was a deal.

One really hard thing about living with a chronic illness is that the effects are relentless. Would I be able to finish the hike? Only time would tell. Was repelling down the cliff safe with the pressure change? Probably. Maybe. I was still going to try it! When I was diagnosed, I knew that I didn't want to live in fear of the disease. I would continue to enjoy life and live spontaneously. Are there changes I've had to make because of the diagnosis? Of course. To this day, I am still learning what my body can and cannot do without regretting it the next morning. Despite the changes though, I continue to live free of fear and refuse to let the disease squash my sense of adventure.

By the grace of God alone, they found my bag and it showed up at the resort in one piece that night. We would be trekking to that cliffside in the morning!

Chris had assured me before we left for the trip that he was capable of packing for himself, so I let him. He apparently didn't think pants would be necessary in the tropics, which I guess is fair. I think he thought he was going to get out of the repelling deal, but Jasper, our guide, offered him a pair of pants. Chris took one look at them and knew he wouldn't even be able to get them halfway up his calves, so he decided to tough it out in less-than-enough coverage. How hard could a walk through the rainforest be after a night of monsoon rain?

We were covered in mud, and more sweat than has ever graced my body at one time, as we came to the summit of the mountain a few hours later. Luckily, we avoided the snakes and jaguars on the way—another reason the guides had insisted Chris wear pants. I decided to go first, but I handed my camera to Jasper so that he could capture the over-the-edge moments. Seeing those pictures now, I'm so glad I did! They had to all but push Chris over the edge, and his face in the pictures showed exactly how he was feeling about that. Once we were both on solid ground again, we shared our exclamations about the rush of repelling down and that thrilling moment when our feet no longer had anything to touch and the rest of the way was as fast as the guide wanted to send us to the ground. So. Much. Fun.

The next leg of our trip was fabulous, as we spent three days either oceanside, poolside, or tableside eating the freshest food. Unfortunately (read: thankfully), I never got to hold up my end of the deal because someone had a very upset stomach the morning of our snorkeling trip (and it wasn't me!). I still have not gone, to this day!

After leaving the Belizean beach, we headed towards Guatemala in a pre-arranged taxi. This driver wasn't an alumnus of the Indy 500, but he got us to the border quickly nonetheless. If you've been to any border crossing in Central America, you're familiar with the lines of taxi drivers who are ready to grab your bags and usher you into their car. "Ignore them and keep walking," I said to Chris as we made our way through the throngs to get our passports stamped. There was a driver waiting for us on the Guatemalan side who didn't have an incorrectly-spelled sign, but did have a suspicious mustache (has there ever been an unsuspicious mustache?) and a very similar hat to our first driver.

Now, if you were surprised that Chris had agreed to repel down a mountain for me (despite his fear of heights, which I may have failed to mention earlier, because, hey, you're supposed to be on my side), you'll be really surprised to hear that he ventured with me to the same cinder block house I had lived in three years prior, without knowing more than a few Spanish words. It was so fun having him see where I had spent my study abroad and meet the people I had come to know and love as family. I spent our days interpreting much of what was being said and relishing in showing off this smiley (because that's who he is, but also because that's the only way he could communicate), loyal man, while assuring all of my Guatemalan mamas that yes, he was *un hombre buenísimo* for their sweet *mija*.

When I said I interpreted "much of what was being said," I chose my words wisely. I did in fact leave out the part when Ron told me that we really needed to be sure to have our passports on us at all times and that even if we did, it might not matter if we got stopped by the militia. Remember the thirty-six year civil war I mentioned earlier? It ended in the nineties, and despite my mother's apprehensions, things had been safe while I had lived there on my own. What I hadn't known prior to this trip was that things had worsened. There was no sense in worrying Chris, so I just didn't translate that part. Thankfully, nothing happened, and we escaped with our lives for the second time on our honeymoon—such a relaxing, joyful time—no, really!

I had commuted from Illinois to Wisconsin for a year, but now that we were married, the goal was to find something closer to home. With that in mind, I had left my high school teaching job at the end of the previous school year. Since the new school year had already started and I had been busy planning a wedding and not applying for jobs, I took that as an opportunity to start my own business. Now, don't read that last sentence and think that I was in any way prepared for this decision. Really, my only qualifications were that I loved making things with my God-given talent, most people liked what I created, and I had a strong sense that if I were to be successful with this, I needed to do everything I could to ensure that my customer was always right. I would put my handmade signs and hand-painted mugs on display for the world to see. Hopefully someone would like them enough to buy them!

I had no formal business training (unless selling lemonade on the corner as an eight-year-old counts—which would then probably qualify most of us) and really no idea what I was doing. Thankfully, I didn't have to pass a job interview, since I would be working for myself. Etsy made it super simple to start an online shop. I think I had three listings (and a lot of hope) the day I went live. To my dismay, it was almost two long months until I made my first sale! I remember complaining and worrying to my husband (*husband!*)

a lot those first weeks, wondering why I wasn't selling anything and doubting my decision to even think I could make this work. How could I think that anyone would want stuff that *I* made?! I've read a multitude of Instagram and blog posts that assure me that I was not alone in those questions. Entrepreneurs and small business owners, especially artists and others who put a piece of themselves into the world, spend hours upon hours wondering how that art will be received. After lots of hard work, I am coming up on the 10th anniversary of opening my shop (and of calling Chris my husband!) and I am grateful I made both of those decisions.

At the time of writing this book, I have just over 2,000 sales, which for me, is a huge milestone! I am thankful for the side hustle and the opportunity I have to bless others with my hand lettering and creative home decor. It's no multi-million dollar company, and I'm still not even sure if I am doing things the "best" way, but I enjoy it and hope to someday quit my day job. For the most part, 99.9% of my customers have actually been right, and the .1% got what they wanted (and a prayer said on their behalf) despite their terrible attitude.

After paying for a wedding, we couldn't afford to have me not making money for long, and since I wasn't getting orders (yet!), I decided to search for a teaching job. Actually, one kinda fell into my lap, thanks to my friend Nik. She was working as a Special Education Classroom Assistant (SECA) at a charter school (I know this idea has been politicized, but the two that I have worked at were fabulous and really offered an amazing education for students who wouldn't have otherwise had anything similar at their neighborhood school) in Chicago. I had taken only one class that touched on special education and most definitely wasn't certified to be a special education classroom teacher, but I was offered the job on the day of my interview! Remember how I explained that God prepares you for where He calls you? Well, I learned a lot that year (even how to clean poop off of a bathroom stall) and loved every second of working with my eight kiddos. They were precious souls; they were so full of life, energy, and love.

About a month after I started that job (around Thanksgiving) my legs started swelling pretty severely. Knowing this was a symptom that presents itself in many children with lymphangiomatosis, we made an appointment with Dr. K. After looking at some imaging, he wasn't entirely convinced that it was related to the disease process and therefore wasn't willing to start treatment, so we didn't.

Disappointingly, the swelling worsened to the point where it was difficult and even painful to walk. I had one (work-appropriate) pair of shoes that fit when the edema was at its worst, and even then, the strap on the mary janes had to be undone or on its last notch. The clunky, cantankerous elevator in our super old, three story building in the city, was a preferred option to hiking up six flights of stairs.

My attitude remained steadfast and joyful at work, as I maintained a smile with my colleagues and students. At home, I also chose joy as often as possible. With any uncomfortable, chronic situation though, even for the happiest of the happy, there are days. You know them. The kind where "it just doesn't seem fair," and crying is truly the only option. "Why is this happening to me?" "When will I be able to wear normal shoes again or walk up the stairs without pain?" I 100% recognize that swollen feet and calves aren't the end of the world, but chronic edema weighs you down (literally–haha).

Through the hard days and the less hard days, I continued to work through five-year-olds' tantrums and eight-year-olds' gym classes. The school I was working at had a college theme that could be seen on its walls and heard in its halls. For example, each classroom was named after a college and even had its own cheer about that college (created by the students, of course!). We had "Community Circle" every Friday where we would all gather in the gym for a celebration of the accomplishments of the week. Each class would do their class cheer, and Specials (art, music, PE) awards were handed out to the classes that exuded the values of pride, success, or honor. It was always such a fun way to end the week, filled with celebration, laughter, and a congratulatory spirit. It was hard to walk away feeling down about life, but one day, in December 2012, I just couldn't get rid of a migraine and therefore was feeling pretty awful.

I headed home a bit early and spent the next few days laying in bed, nauseous and dreading the inevitable: a visit to the ER. We had just recently moved south to Brookfield, IL, so we knew very little about the area. Desperate, Chris googled the nearest hospital, and we headed to the ER in need of relief: he, behind the wheel, and me, with my head propped on pillows in the front seat, reeling with pain, and drowning in the intense pressure in my head and neck. The search had led us to a city hospital in the midst of flu season. The wait was miserable and seemingly interminable. I don't remember much of the three-hour wait, other than laying on the floor, tring to block out all the noise with my hands over my ears. Once I was finally taken back and given some fluids and pain meds, my head started to clear.

The second diagnosis of meningitis came after the dreaded lumbar puncture, and I was swiftly admitted to a room with two beds. This is not a pleasant nor an ideal situation for anyone involved. I remember being separated only by a curtain, and the poor lady next to us had bowel issues and had to use the latrine literally two feet away from us. As I suffered there with nausea and a migraine, I kindly asked to be moved to a private room, but that wasn't an option. In that small room, we were left with more questions than answers as we began to wonder if there was a connection between meningitis and lymphangiomatosis. Was I more susceptible to the disease due to my other medical complications? The doctors didn't have much to say, so the questions lingered.

The nurse came in to put a port in my arm so that, once I

returned home, I could continue to administer the strong antibiotics that were battling for my life. I am a petite person, but finding my veins has never really been a problem. She fumbled through her explanation of the possibility of infection with the port, as she used my body as a table for her sterile equipment and pricked me three times, each time ending in failure. With each failed attempt, I gave my best rah rah pep talk and steadied myself for the next intravenous (hopefully) attack. After the third pathetic attempt, I politely asked for someone else to try. Days earlier, I had endured a similar barrage of failed needle sticks and ended up having an IV put in my hand. If you've ever had to endure that inhumanity, I am sorry! After that, I just wanted someone who could get the job done!

In walked sweet Shirley. Her bouncy curls matched her bubbly personality, and she chit-chatted about this, that, and the other thing as she opened another sterile packet (again laid on my chest) and swiftly inserted the PICC line. Although I was rejoicing in her success rate, I was dreading all that was represented by that port. The peripherally inserted central catheter (PICC) would allow the administration of IV antibiotics to be done in the comfort of my own home, which sounds great, but when it's me giving them to myself, it's a little intimidating!

Respect your nurses—their jobs are hard and
their hearts are in the right place.

Trying to get over my fear, I listened acutely as Shirley explained the step-by-step process of administering the medication. The medicine is delivered via a long tube attached on one end to a soft plastic ball about twice the size of a baseball and on the other to the PICC line Shirley had just inserted. The balls must be kept refrigerated until the medicine is to be administered over an extended period of time (I believe with my dose it was between thirty and forty-five minutes). Syringes filled with heparin (to avoid blood clots) and saline, as well as a box of alcohol pads accompanied the fascinating, round apparatus that allowed medicine to be administered by the patients themselves.

My next task, before having to worry about any of those steps, was to have a bowel movement. Having to discuss so many personal things in the hospital, with straight up strangers, is rather annoying. You get to the point where it's not even embarrassing anymore, and somehow being asked by someone you've met one time if you've had a bowel movement yet, is mundane. Yes, you've seen me half naked, you've helped me go to the bathroom, you've cleaned up my vomit, why not also discuss how many times I have or have not excreted waste from my poorly functioning body. And then there is the celebration once it does happen. It's the moment everyone has been waiting for, and once it happens, the light turns green, and you're able to start your discharge paperwork (whenever the nurse gets around to it, of course).

Now, don't get me wrong, I am not knocking nurses. There are many nurses in my life whom I love dearly, and I know they work their butts off, but I've never been treated by any of them. There has yet to be a time where once my body is cleared for departure, the landing wheels are released swiftly. This occasion was no different. We spent the next eight hours watching Flip or Flop on HGTV and waiting to be released.

But He was pierced
for our rebellion,
crushed for our sins.
He was beaten
so we could be whole.
He was whipped
so we could be healed.

Isaiah 53:5
nlt

Experience Your Joys and Pains as Your Own

I know there are worse things than swollen feet, and there is always someone who hurts more, has to try harder, or gets less than what they deserve after working so hard, but I also know that it's not really fair to compare yourself to others—in your joy or your pain. My pain (or joy) isn't any less or more painful (or joyful) to me because someone else is experiencing different pain (or joy). This is something that I hope you can come to understand (if you haven't already).

This is not to say that there are no injustices that are worth fighting against. There are most definitely things that happen in this broken world that need solutions, but that discussion is not why we are here. All I am saying is that it is important to empathize with each other as humans. Accepting and embracing others' pain and joy can help us support and celebrate one another. It avoids the comparison game, which is better for everyone!

Moment for Reflection

How can you remind yourself that your competition is yourself and not those around you? Write a post-it (or two, or ten) and stick them around your house, in the book you're currently reading, on your dashboard, etc. so that you can be reminded often.

10

Kidney Malfunction

She was nice enough, as she sat on the edge of our couch. Her bag was filled with anything she might need; everything in its specific compartment. We talked like old friends as she ran the tests. The pause in conversation caused me to notice the panicked look on her face. "You need to get to the ER immediately. Your numbers are too high." Since my discharge from the hospital over a week ago, I had been administering the antibiotic vancomycin myself, but Rita, the home health nurse, came twice a week to check my blood. Her concern was contagious, so we gathered some items for a quick overnight bag (just in case) and headed out the door after thanking her for her diligence.

As we rang in the new year (another one in the hospital), we waited patiently for the diagnosis. It was hard to muster even the faintest hint of glee, despite the fanfare, excitement, and around-the-globe firework displays on the tiny television hanging in the corner. Shortly after 12:30, a new doctor walked in. He awkwardly made a joke about the singers on Dick Clark's Rockin' New Years Eve as Chris grabbed my hand. After our feeble attempts to humor him, he introduced himself as Doctor Ruman, the resident kidney doctor. He explained how my kidneys appeared as if they were giving up their filtering role, so my blood was filled with more than what it could handle. It wasn't much of an explanation in terms of why it was happening, or even what the prognosis was, but we knew that I wouldn't have to stay much longer than the night. We thanked him, wished him a happy 2013, and watched him slowly walk away.

By the time we had left the hospital, the world was in a new year, functioning at normal capacity, unlike my kidneys. I attended my follow up appointment with Dr. Lee the following week. I met with his intern first. All I wanted was someone to tell me what was going on, and all he wanted was to know if I had any edema. Of course I did, but my blood pressure was fine, so he went to get the doctor. Dr. Lee walked briskly into the room with his disheveled, wispy white hair fluttering to the side. His expression was kind, if a bit rushed. He rubbed his white goatee and offered an explanation that was only a tad more thorough than the one from the doctor we had met on New Years Eve. It left us questioning what this diagnosis meant and why it had suddenly appeared. The official diagnosis of "nephrotic kidney disease" literally means "we're just not sure" what caused your kidneys to stop functioning properly. At this point, I knew that something had damaged my kidneys pretty badly, and if they continued to worsen, I would be spending some time tethered to a dialysis machine each week. When we asked about the future, he motioned his hands through the air as if chopping up a zucchini and used simple fractions: ⅓ of the people stay the same, ⅓ of the people get worse, and ⅓ of the people get better.

I was going to get better. I had to be the last fraction, I thought, as I silently whispered a prayer while Chris asked him a few more questions. What were the treatment options? How bad was it *really*? Would I eventually need dialysis? Dr. Lee set forth a plan for the next three months: stop eating fast food (I rarely ate it anyway), lower your salt intake (Mrs. Dash it is!), and take your blood pressure every day. The numbers showed that it was, indeed, pretty dire, but he was hopeful that with the aforementioned plan I wouldn't need dialysis within the next six months. There was a trial that he was trying to get the hospital board to approve that was being run at Mayo Clinic, and he thought I would be a good candidate. Before that though, he wanted a kidney biopsy to see if there was anything he was missing.

"I'm sure it has something to do with my lymphangiomatosis." I said, a little bit hoping that it did. At least that would be an explanation for why a young twenty-something suddenly had kidney disease.

"Yeah, explain that to me again. What do you have?" questioned Dr. Lee as he perused my chart looking for clues.

Of course he had never heard of it. Most doctors hadn't. I explained the extra lymph pockets that were causing my bones to disappear and how the disease lowered my immune system. He had suggested tacrolimus as a potential treatment option. It sounded awfully similar to sirolimus, which my oncologist had suggested, so I implored him to speak with Dr. K. He waved his fingers and nodded his head, as if to say he didn't really need to and that he'd research on his own. How did I get all that from his body language? I had seen it before.

Less than two weeks later, I rested on the edge of my seat. The ultrasound tech called my name and led me down a very chilly hallway, lit with the cool fluorescents of the hospital. The room she brought me to was tiny, with only the space for a bed and an ultrasound machine. She handed me a gown as she walked out and let me know she would knock when she returned.

Already freezing, I quickly changed into the gown that would provide no warmth. The tech returned with the doctor, introduced us, and departed shortly after. She had kind eyes, which was comforting since that's all I could really see above her mask. Doctor Temps explained the process and assured me it wouldn't take long. I held stealthily still, which wasn't difficult, because I was practically frozen by that point anyway. Thankfully, the ultrasound goop was warm as the probe roamed across my body to find my kidney. She located it, and inserted the needle a few times to gather more than one sample of the failing tissue. It was over before I knew it and I hastily changed into my slightly warmer clothes and headed home.

The biopsy results were normal. In most cases, this is a good thing. In cases where your body is riddled with nonsense, sometimes it's easier to hear negative results that will at least lead to an explanation for all the unusual things. I had more questions: was it possible they just didn't pull the tissue from the right spot? Could there be lymph involvement in another location around my kidney? If the results were normal, what had caused the sudden malfunction? Possibly. Unlikely. No idea. Those were the doctor's [slightly paraphrased] responses to my questions. We did entertain the thought that because I had taken Excedrin Migraine almost every day for at least the last twelve years, my kidneys were finally calling it quits. At that point, there had been no long-term studies completed on the effects of acetaminophen on the body, let alone on the kidneys. The amount I was taking was definitely not healthy, but it's all that seemed to help me live a somewhat "normal" life. As it were, I often spent time secluded in a dark room somewhere, sleeping or waiting for the pain of the headache to subside, even after taking the medicine.

For the next year, the swelling in my legs continued to worsen, but my dismal numbers stayed relatively the same. I wasn't getting better, but I wasn't getting worse. I continued to eat as healthy as I could and pray that my kidneys would improve. I knew God was in the miracle business, so I was trusting Him. At the same time, I had come to learn that it's also important that I do my best to care for my body: mentally, physically, and spiritually. The diet didn't seem to have much of an effect, but it couldn't have been hurting, so we stayed away from salt as much as possible. We continued to invest in our church family and reap the benefits of their investment in us. We prayed for God's guidance on our medical journey. I also prayed for a new job.

In the early part of spring in 2014, I hadn't seen any improvement with the daily swelling. I had pitting edema in both my calves and my shins that left me literally "kicking my feet up" at the end of each day. My numbers hadn't gotten better in that first year, but they hadn't worsened either. It seemed I may have been part of the first fraction—the one that stays the same. At that point, I was choosing happiness and thanking Jesus for the fact that I hadn't needed to start dialysis! Unfortunately, three months later, my blood was telling a bit of a different story.

My liver had the bright idea to start producing an overwhelming amount of cholesterol, since my kidneys were still out of whack. Now, not only was I in my mid-twenties with kidney disease, I was now on Lipitor and a diuretic. If you had read my chart, and skipped over my birthdate, you may have thought I was an eighty-five-year-old woman. Despite the downturn, I was doing alright. The hospital still hadn't decided to start the trial, but it was looking like starting treatment might be a good option, so Dr. Lee started preparing me for the possibility of entering the trial. He put me on losartan to keep my blood pressure from climbing too high, at the risk of light-headedness and fainting. It seems that medicine is always a delicate balancing act, and thankfully, for the moment, I probably could have tight-roped across the Rio Grande.

Medicine can help, but it can also act as a band-aid and can prevent an opportunity for true healing. Be sure to take it only when that's your best option.

In my professional life, I was about to head in a different direction. On my way home from work, sitting in the bumper-to-bumper traffic that is Chicago city driving, a song came on the radio. It was a song that I had only heard a few times before, but this time, it seemed as if it was speaking directly to me. Maybe you've had that experience before, and maybe you haven't. If you have, you know what I'm talking about. Anyway, it was a song called "Oceans," by Hillsong. There is a line in the song that says,

> "You call me out upon the waters,
> The great unknown,
> where feet may fail.
> And there I find you in the mystery …"

It was another one of those moments. God was calling me to do something that I didn't really seem prepared for; it definitely didn't seem that great of a time for it, and I didn't really want to do it. I was starting to learn from my previous experiences that He wouldn't lead me astray. So, I walked into my principal's office the next morning and shared with her that I would be leaving at the end of the school year. Of course, I had shared my Spirit-prompted thoughts with my husband before finalizing the decision, and he had agreed with my conclusion.

Did I have a job lined up? No. Was I aware of where I would be, come the fall? No. Did I know for certain that God would provide and honor my obedience? Absolutely. My faith was strong in that moment. God had continued to show up time and again in my life, and I was fairly confident that the Sovereign King of the universe could handle finding a job for little ol' me. Afterall, if He had prompted me to leave Rowe, I could trust that He had a reason for it.

If God calls you to do it, He will provide the way to get it done.

Over the next two months, I went to several interviews. Up until this point, I had never *not* gotten a job that I interviewed for.

That didn't cause any cockiness, but more of a confidence during interviews. That quickly changed, as I received rejection call after rejection call. I was maybe starting to question my "calling" to leave my previous school just a teensy bit. Our school year didn't end until the second week in June, so I was still teaching and getting paid as my ego took a few more hits.

The end of May arrived, and I interviewed at a great school. The interview went really well—at least *I* thought it had. I remember coming home and sharing with Chris that this one may be the one. The next day, the principal called to share that the teacher that was previously in the position had decided to not move away and would therefore be staying in her role. Happy for her, but sad for me, I prayed a simple prayer: "Father, I know you are in control. Please show me where You need me to be."

AppliTrack and I had been spending a lot of time together, and that night was no different. An application for a bilingual resource teacher in Round Lake popped up on the screen. Sure, it was over an hour away, but it seemed like a great fit! I would be pulling small groups of students and would be able to use my Spanish, which was something I had been hoping and praying for. I started filling out the application, but got called away from my computer, although I don't remember for what, and it doesn't much matter. I would get back to it when I had the time.

Later that week, my phone started ringing. I have a habit of not answering calls from numbers I don't know, but I noticed the location of the call was Round Lake. Oh no! I hadn't finished that application, I thought. Curious though, I answered. The lady on the other end of the line sounded cheerful, yet a bit overwhelmed. It was mid-June, and the teacher-candidate pool didn't have many options left at that point, so I understood her misery. I was on the other end of that conundrum as available positions seemed to be disappearing by the day. She acknowledged that I had left the application incomplete and questioned if I was still interested in the position. Flabbergasted, I responded, maybe too quickly, with an overzealous "yes!" My haste pleased her, so we scheduled the interview for the following week.

We chatted like old friends, in that dank olive green building; ones whose interests included language acquisition and ensuring students have the best opportunity for growth. Sitting behind a desk covered in disheveled papers, she smiled a genuine smile. "I think you are exactly what we are looking for. I will chat with my team and get back to you soon." Graciously, I thanked her as I made my way to the door and into the hot June sunshine. For the second time in a few short months, I felt that this might be the job. The first time, though, I was wrong.

My feelings proved me right that afternoon, as I tentatively accepted the position of bilingual resource teacher over the phone. The human resources department made the day even better when they shared my salary, which was almost $20,000 more than I had been making in my previous position! With that delightful news in mind, I prayed a prayer of thanksgiving: for a new job that aligned with my passion for teaching language and that would definitely help us financially as we were in the market for a home. I shared the information with Chris, and we celebrated God's provision. The only thing that wasn't ideal was the fact that we lived over an hour away from Round Lake.

The first two months in my position were full of learning and driving. Thankfully, the week before school started, we had our offer accepted for a house in Palatine which would be almost exactly halfway between Chris' job and my new one. Unfortunately, we didn't close until September 30th, which meant my commute would provide a challenge. Early mornings aren't something my body handles well. People with GLA (generalized lymphatic anomalies), or lymphangiomatosis as it was previously diagnosed as, will tell you the importance of maintaining a consistent sleep schedule, including an ample amount of sleep. In order to adjust for my body's needs, I ended up spending a few nights a week at SBB's house in Buffalo Grove, which cut my commute in half. It was fun to spend some extra time with my college roommate and her husband, but living out of my car three days a week and not seeing Chris every night was a bit rough.

The closing date came, and we anxiously accepted the keys to our very first home. Chris' mom was our realtor, and she made the process as simple as buying your first home could be! As grateful as we were to finally be in our house, we weren't as excited about the cleaning. I don't know about you, but I am of the opinion that cleaning other people's messes is just about one of the last things I want to spend my time doing. I commend housekeeping teams around the world that do that day in and day out, because it is extremely unpleasant. Although, I'm sure their job does not entail scrubbing layers of nicotine off of wooden doors and vacuuming up clumps of cat hair from above the kitchen cabinets. Disgusting. I am not a cat person, am highly allergic to them, and could not have been more grossed out thinking about the previous owners' cats laying on top of what were now our kitchen cabinets.

Along with the cat hair and the nicotine, came smelly carpets. We tore them out and were pleasantly surprised to find hardwood floors in the master bedroom. When we had asked about the potential for hardwood in that room, the sellers shot down our hopes. Well, they had also told us they didn't smoke in the house, but the wads of brown rags and need for two coats of primer on all the walls negated that promise.

After two weeks of endless nights, lots of driving, frozen meals, and help from my in-laws, our house was finally move-in ready! We were thrilled with how it had turned out and loved the location! Neither of us had really been to Palatine before, so we had a new village to explore! Plus, there was a huge Hobby Lobby right down the street, and my commute to work was cut almost in half. I was also now reverse commuting, meaning the heavy traffic was coming toward me instead of crawling along with me. All good things.

On top of all that goodness, my job was turning out to be such a blessing! I was working with almost seventy kids in small groups (which is A LOT), but they were so hardworking and willing to learn, that it made it worth the long hours of planning. The staff members at the school were passionate and caring and made going to work every day fun! God had clearly known what He was doing.

My swelling had somewhat improved. It was no longer hard to fit into my shoes, and I could pull most of my pants past my knees. The fall visit to the kidney doctor left me a little discouraged though. My numbers hadn't really improved, despite the improvement in my physical symptoms. Dr. Lee was still trying to get the trial approved and confirmed that I would still be a strong candidate. We discussed the option of starting me on rituximab without waiting for the trial to see if my albumin or proteinuria would respond. Chris and I decided that it wouldn't hurt to try, so Dr. Lee sent me home with a twenty-four-hour urine collection jug and asked that I return it the next day.

The results of the sample didn't garner any special conclusions. Therefore, Dr. Lee talked us through what rituximab treatment would entail. It was an infusion that I would have to take once a month for several hours. Since its primary goal is to reduce the number of immune cells in the body in order to lower the chance for inflammation, it would suppress my immune system. I would have to take extra precautions—especially working with my students.

Since I had just started my new job, I spent some time praying that my boss would be compassionate about this and that HR would cooperate. Our principal, Dr. Fair, wore three-inch heels every day and drove a Harley on the weekends. For some reason, I was a little intimidated. As I was wringing my hands during our conversation, she graciously reminded me that my health should come before my work and that she would do whatever she could to ensure that my role was not thwarted by the necessity of this medicine. She kept her promise, and the next few months continued well.

I can't quite remember the reasoning, but I never did start the infusions. I think it was due to an insurance delay, and by the time we heard back (a few months later), my numbers were starting to drastically improve. The use of the word drastic may be a bit of a stretch. I wasn't completely out of the woods, and Dr. Lee couldn't promise that I wouldn't need dialysis someday or even that the swelling would go away. When you're a person with chronic, nephrotic kidney disease though, ANY improvement in the number seems like cause for celebration, so that's what we did!

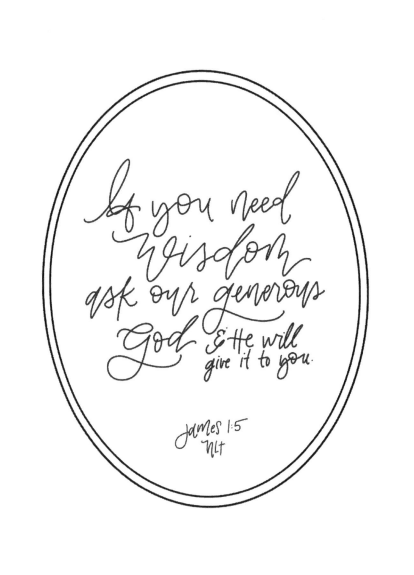

If you need
wisdom
ask our generous
God & He will
give it to you.

James 1:5
NLT

An Expert Patient

As a person with a couple of rare illnesses, I've learned the importance of advocating for oneself. One thing that I've disliked about those illnesses is the undeniable guarantee that I will know more about my disease than my doctor. It's just a fact of life. It wasn't Dr. Lee's fault that he had never heard of lymphangiomatosis. My primary doctor could not be blamed for treating me like a lab rat to be studied and even suggesting she use my case for a journal article. I'm used to the "guinea pig" status as well as the look of novelty on each new doctor's face, but it doesn't make it any easier.

Doctors are supposed to be the experts. When you need a medical explanation, a treatment plan, or a prognosis, the doc should be the one to offer it. In my case, it hasn't really ever been that way. I've walked into a doctor's office with two typed pages of my medical history so that 1. I don't forget, and 2. they can keep it once I leave.

It's not easy being an expert on your own body. Most people won't believe you. Most people will give you the advice they think is right (based on their bodies). Most people won't understand. Most people will judge you, call you lazy, or wonder why they can't "see" your symptoms. Find the ones who do believe you, keep their advice to themselves, do understand, and aren't judging you. Those are the good ones. The ones who will offer to pick up groceries when you've had a three-day migraine or listen to stories about your miraculous healing and celebrate with you. And–*and*–when you find the doctor who listens intently, tries to understand, commits to researching your unique symptoms and disease, acknowledges that they don't know it all, and needs to be *one part* of your medical team—hold on to them and don't let go.

If you haven't found your people yet, keep looking—they're out there somewhere! It took me twenty three years to find a doctor who admitted that I wasn't losing it. Until then, keep telling your story.

11

Change of Plans

"They haven't agreed to start the trial yet, but the good news is that you don't qualify for it anymore anyway."

What did he just say? I stared, with my bottom jaw practically on the floor, as I listened to Dr. Lee spout off my numbers like he was an auctioneer. Somehow, despite skipping rituximab, my kidneys were filtering things pretty well again. The holes in my "filters" weren't quite as small as they should be, so I was still leaking some protein and swelling a bit in my legs, but I would take it!

When the medicine trial doesn't work out, it's probably a blessing. Don't try to make it happen. That doesn't just pertain to medicine trials.

2015 had started off strong. My kidney function continued to improve, and my swelling was almost insignificant by the end of the summer. I still had migraines for more than half of every month, and the sweltering Chicago heat wasn't helping. I had learned over the years that my body doesn't handle extremes well: neither too hot nor too cold. I prefer a slightly breezy 72°F. I also had learned over the years that living my life symptom free was probably not a realistic expectation, and I was grateful that I had mostly just dealt with them. Reminding myself of how bad it had been in the past provided a daily opportunity for joy and thanksgiving.

That August, Chris and I met with my oncologist to update him on the positive progress we had seen over the past year. He celebrated with us about the news. Our next conversation wasn't as fun. Since I was doing so well, Chris and I had planned to discuss our options when it came to pregnancy. Knowing that the disease tends to worsen with hormonal changes, we were less than hopeful that his words would be any more promising than they were. At this point, Dr. K hadn't worked with any pregnant women that had lymphangiomatosis. In his treatment group, which included doctors from Spain and a couple other European countries, as well as several across the U.S., he had heard of only eight women with this disease who had had babies. That wasn't a very big sample size, but nevertheless, those results were the only thing we had. Doctors had reported that some of the women had actually improved during pregnancy, but all of them had relapsed or seen a worsening of symptoms postpartum.

His next words left me in tears through lunch and most of the rest of the hour-long drive home. We didn't receive an outright, "no, you shouldn't try to get pregnant," but Dr. K gently urged us that maybe adoption would be a good option. Now, I had nothing against adoption. Matter of fact, Chris and I had talked about adopting after having a child or two through my own pregnancies. It didn't matter that the response wasn't a blatant "no." I trusted Dr. K, knew he had my best interests in mind, and to my ears, I was hearing a resounding, "natural pregnancy is not an option."

Of course we had thanked Dr. K for sharing his thoughts with us in such a kind way. We had also discussed the treatment options for if I did choose to go the natural pregnancy route. At the time, I wasn't on any preventative or maintenance medication for the lymph disease, but I was still on losartan, which wasn't really an issue. He referred me to a high-risk gynecologist and told me he would support whatever decision we made.

My appointment with the high-risk OBGYN didn't leave me

feeling any more confident in a decision to try to get pregnant. She really had no knowledge of my lymph disease and stated she was more concerned about my kidneys and the potential for hypertension and/or preeclampsia. Not to mention that women who do not have issues with swelling prepartum, often develop them while pregnant. For all of you reading this who have had a baby through your own pregnancy, I hope you recognize the amazing thing your body has done for you and all that you had to endure is nothing short of a miracle. Pregnancy is rough on a woman's body, and if that woman has several other health concerns, without strong knowledge on how they may be affected, pregnancy seems a little scary. The other consideration was my health once the baby was born. Would I be healthy enough to care for it? Would my symptoms worsen to the point of needing treatment that would lower my quality of life as well as hurt my already suffering immune system? Would the burden of an ailing wife and a newborn be overwhelming for Chris?

The next few months were filled with moments of contentment. They were also filled with moments of intense grief. That's the annoying thing about grief. At first, it's everywhere you look. After some time, it starts showing up when you least expect it. Like that annoying neighbor who always tries to peer in your windows, or the person who cuts you off on the highway at high speeds. You feel like you're cruising along, doing well, and then BAM! Out of nowhere, the red Mercedes of grief practically sideswipes you and you're left with a puddle of tears and dashed hopes again.

Not only was I dealing with the unannounced grief visits, I was also struggling with feeling like I was making a selfish decision. If we chose not to pursue a pregnancy because of my own health being put in jeopardy, would that make me selfish? I sought out the wisdom of friends and family that spoke truth into my life.

"It is definitely not selfish to choose your health over a baby."
"You need to ensure that you are healthy enough
to care for a baby once it's here."
"Adoption is a beautiful thing and will lead to the same result."
"You and Chris can have a beautiful baby through
adoption that you will love as your own."
"Adoption is a picture of the gospel and is love exemplified."

I didn't have much of a problem listening to the words of my sweet friends and family, but it took me several months to believe them.

I can tell you that I now spend the majority of my days in the "belief camp" on this one. I am grateful for the words of encouragement and the daily dose of prayer that leave me knowing we made the right decision for our family given the circumstances. I will mention that at the writing of this, five years have passed, so I've had time to sit with that decision and continue to thank God for His provision. Big life decisions aren't always easy to make, and they don't always provide satisfaction right away. That doesn't mean it was the wrong decision. It most likely means that God is still working on you.

That fall, as I was working through all of those feelings I just discussed, I spent the weekend with some friends/coworkers at a conference at my friend's church. Speaker after speaker urged us to share our stories in a way that would honor God's work in our lives and provide opportunities to bring Him glory. We had time to practice sharing our story with perfect strangers. At the time, this was terrifying and exhilarating. Looking back, I can clearly see that it was God preparing me for what was to come. Coming off the conference high, I was prompted to share a few weeks later during an open mic session at my church. These sessions are few and far between, but this one was heavenly-timed. It seemed ridiculous to me that I would stand and speak to the church about my kidney function and how it seemed like my kidneys were improving and that God was clearly at work. Despite the ridiculousness, God used my words to encourage those around me and remind them that we serve a God who heals. I have had several people (many of whom I had never spoken to before) approach me since I shared and tell me how grateful they were for my story and how helpful it was to hear the words I spoke that day.

It is important to note that we don't always recognize our own bravery. Many people over the years have said, "You are *so* brave!" which was extremely awkward and uncomfortable for me. I didn't agree with them for a long time, and let me tell you why. My response was simply, "I had to do it." I felt that I didn't have a choice in the matter. If my body was hurting, I needed to seek the necessary help in order to get better (even if that meant seeking it for a very long time). I had to get up and live my life every day. What I didn't realize about my actions was that I was making the choice to be joyful through it all and to put my trust in Jesus. Without really reflecting on it, I assumed those were the only options.

I have always been a positive person about everything, not just my health. It wasn't until one of my coworkers pointed out that it was incredible how happy I was despite my circumstances, that I took a second to recognize the choice I had in all of it. I could have spent my days crying in my room, being angry at God, and being rude or mean to those around me out of feelings of resentment. I wasn't doing any of those things; what a miserable life that would be! Of course, there were times that I did cry about my situation, and even question God's reasoning for what I had to endure, but those were few and far between. Sure, I had a few rare diseases that I had no control over, but I wasn't about to let them change who I was or what I was all about. I would continue seeking adventures, loving those around me, and telling people about the great things God had done in my life.

You have a choice every day. We all have struggles and circumstances that seem dire, but it is how we respond to those that make us into the person we are. Our actions speak to those around us; what are yours saying?

In your hearts
honor Christ
the LORD as holy,
always being
prepared to make a
defense to
anyone who asks
you for a reason
for the HOPE
that is in you;
yet do it with
GENTLENESS &
RESPECT.

1 Peter 3:15
ESV

Share Your Story

The most powerful and freeing lesson I've learned in the eight years since God called me to write this book is that: my story doesn't only belong to me, but to the author of it, who is God himself. He is the author and finisher of my story, and because of that, He receives the glory when I share about what He has done and is doing in my life.

I definitely consider myself a relational evangelist. You wouldn't find me on the street corner with a megaphone and a perfectly hand-lettered sign about God's faithfulness. Nor would you catch me handing out tracts at the mall (do people even shop in person anymore?) or sending them to unbelievers in the mail. It's even weird for me that this book has found its way into your hands by the grace of God, but I hope that it feels like we know each other. That it is written in such a way that you feel as if we are sharing a sweet conversation over a cuppa something. That it doesn't sound like a stranger simply proclaiming what she thinks is good news, but rather a friend sharing her heart and the importance of the Good News of Jesus.

One thing about sharing your story as a way of testifying to the power of Jesus is that it is irrefutable. No one can deny what has happened to you or naysay your experience with God's saving, amazing grace. Hear this: I am not saying "speak your truth," as so many these days shout. Truth is truth and is not impacted by whether I believe it or not. The truth of the gospel is no different today than it was 2,000 years ago when Jesus walked this earth. How amazing is that?! So, I'm not saying that you can call whatever you want, "truth." I am simply saying that your experience can be used as an undeniable witness to God's work in your life.

That said, you don't have to write a book. Take some time today (five minutes to start) and write about how God has changed your life. Then, share what you wrote with someone close to you. I was going to say, "If you feel comfortable–" but it's probably going to be uncomfortable at first. It always is. So, in your uncomfort, share your story. God will get the glory!

12

Remission

Reading through the Old Testament, I'm sure you've found yourself wondering at the incessant, monotonous, obviously ridiculous plight of the Israelites. Time and again they forgot all of the amazing things the Lord had done for them and started worshiping other gods. I have definitely questioned how they could walk away from or deny a God that so willingly parted a sea for them, delivered them from slavery, saved them from a flood, continuously pursued them, and outright loved them. Well, I am not unlike the Israelites, and I'm guessing you're not either. I've already admitted to a handful of times that I had first said "no" to a God request, and *spoiler alert* I will write about a few more before the end of this book. This next one is a big one.

Since I could remember, I had prayed for my dad's salvation. Often that prayer sounded something like this, "Dear heavenly father, thank you for my dad. Please put someone in his life who will share the gospel with him. I pray that he will turn his heart toward you and recognize his need for a savior." I was feeling rather convicted about that prayer as I realized that for almost a quarter of a century I had been praying that God would put *someone else* in my dad's life that would tell him about Jesus. I grappled with the fact that I had never had a conversation with my dad about my own faith or how I knew that Jesus was real and that He was still in the miracle business. God was clearly working on my heart and showing me the importance of having this conversation. Of course, I had another Israelite moment and tried to suppress the prompting for several months.

I continued to hear God's still small voice. After months of justifying my rebellion with the phrase, "someone else will tell him," I decided to call my dad. He was living in Texas, and I hadn't seen him for a while. We talked about the heat there and the lack of it in Chicago. We talked about our pets and jobs. We talked about the traffic. When we had exhausted all the mundane topics, my heart was racing and my palms were sweating. I silently pleaded to God for the right words and then I dove in. We talked about things that mattered: like, faith and why my father couldn't seem to believe in a God he couldn't see. We also talked about the divorce and why my dad had left all of those years ago. Miracles were also discussed and I explained how I knew that God was the Creator of the universe. At one point, my dad apologized for how he had treated my mom and us kids, and I forgave him: outloud. I had just let go of fifteen-year-old pain and frustation. We ended the call regretfully not being able to hug it out, and even though my dad didn't have a come-to-Jesus moment, I knew that I had planted a seed.

Ultimately, I am not in control of my dad's salvation—it would be rather laughable if we believed we have any power over whether another human being believes in the saving grace of Jesus. All we can do is present the facts, share our story, and let God do the real work.

Relieved about finally having that conversation, I was able to move on to the next big thing: my three-year kidney checkup. It had been *three years* of diuretics, cholesterol medication, and swollen legs. As I handed Chris my purse and jacket to step on the scale, something I had done one hundred times before, I remembered Dr. Lee's words from that first appointment: "one-third of my patients stay the same, one-third get worse, and one-third get better." Then, the words from a more recent appointment played in my mind: "I've never seen anyone go into remission after the first year."

I had been feeling much better, and my swelling had improved pretty drastically. Lots of family members and friends were praying for me, and I was hopeful that we were going to hear good news that day. My numbers had to be at least a little improved from our last visit six months prior. Lost in thought, I answered all of the resident's questions. He felt my legs and commented on the lack of edema and charted that my blood pressure was normal, which was definitely noteworthy.

After a long wait, and a boring game of I Spy (not much to spy in a sterile clinic room), Dr. Lee came in beaming; his grin, filled with crooked, somewhat yellowed teeth practically gave him away. His resident followed closely, also smiling.

"Your lab results are startling and rather unexpected." As Dr. Lee went over my numbers, he finished with a mouthful of the most delightful words I've ever heard, "it seems you're in remission." He was flabbergasted, and I probably floored him with my attribution that followed.

"I've had a lot of people praying for me, and this is pretty clearly a miracle."

He gave a slightly uncomfortable giggle, shifted his glance, and then turned back to face me. "At any rate, I am happy to say I am pleasantly surprised by your improvement. Like I said, I have never seen anyone go into remission from nephrotic kidney disease after a year's time has passed, but here you are after three years."

We discussed the real consequences of the remission and the likelihood of the disease returning. He couldn't tell me with any certainty, since he hadn't seen it before (nor read about it in any journals), but he didn't think it was very likely to cause any more problems, although there was a chance. I should continue to watch my diet, but other than that, I could stop my diuretic and the cholesterol medication.

Chris and I thanked him for his kindness and support over the last three years, and I made a one-year follow-up appointment on the way out. As we returned to the car, I was thanking the Lord and seemingly walking on air. Maybe it was just that I wasn't walking on water anymore, with the lack of swelling in my legs. Since Chris usually met me at the hospital during the work day, he typically drove back to work after a swift goodbye. This time, we decided to celebrate a bit before his return. A quick Target/Starbucks run would have to do. As silly as it is, I remember buying teddy grahams and giddily discussing the miracle over hot drinks. Simple, but sweet. We were just so thankful for the work that God had done and how His glory had been displayed.

Respect the prognosis, but never give up *hope*.
Jesus is still performing miracles.

FAITH

shows the reality of what we

HOPE

for; it is the evidence of things we cannot see.

Hebrews 11:1
NLT

Hope

The word *hope* is littered throughout our daily conversations.

"Are you going to make it into that college?"

"I *hope* so!"

"Is it going to rain this weekend?"

"I *hope* not!"

"I *hope* you like root beer, because that's all they have to drink."

In English, we have watered down the meaning of this word and somehow associated it with doubt or insignificant things that are out of our control like the weather or whether or not something may or may not happen. Contrarily, the Bible speaks of a very different definition of *hope*. In Hebrews 11:1, the author writes about confidence in hope. 1 Peter tells us to be ready to defend the *hope* we have in us as followers of Christ. That kind of *hope* speaks of blessed assurance and a faith that is secure and sure. As Christians, our *hope* is in Christ (Colossians 1:27, ESV). What an amazing thing it is to have this type of promise!

Biblical hope is something I have clung to throughout my medical journey. My faith is secure in the hope of Jesus, and beyond that, nothing matters nearly as much. With this *hope*, we wait with joy and full confidence and rest in the fact that God is a promise keeper.

Moment for Reflection

1. In what or whom does your hope rest?

    _____
    _____
    _____
    _____
    _____
    _____

13

Meningitis – again

2016 was coming right along, and God was clearly at work. It's rather pointless to write that, since He is always at work, even when we can't see it, but when we *can* see it, I believe we should tell people about it. So, here I am, writing to you about it. Hopefully you'll share my story, as well as your own, so that people can hear the impressive story of miracles that God is writing in this world.

March is about the time in schools when the administrators start telling their staff about their plans for the next school year, and this March was no different. My principal approached me with an unlikely proposition: teach bilingual third grade the following school year. I had never been an elementary classroom teacher and wasn't actually trained to be one. To be honest, I was terrified. Sure, I had worked with elementary-aged kids for four years at that point, but I really had no confidence in my ability to manage a classroom full of them for an entire day. I loved the small group environment and seeing many students throughout the day. On the other hand, I really missed teaching math and using my Spanish, so it seemed like a good way to satisfy those cravings.

A couple weeks of convincing, and some prayer was all it took. I accepted the position and began to mentally prepare myself for having my own classroom—so many decorating ideas! I spent most of the summer solidifying a plan for my room, gathering supplies, and preparing to teach third grade. The other part of the summer I spent in Kentucky with a group of high schoolers.

The trip to Appalachia was eye-opening. I was aware of the existence of extreme poverty in the States, but hadn't really witnessed it. I spent my days back in the holler (literally) putting in a french drain for a lady who lived in a double-wide trailer at the bottom of a big hill. Each spring, more and more of her land eroded with the rains. The french drain was supposed to prohibit that from continuing by redirecting the water to a different area through a pipe lying in a gravel-filled trench.

There were four or five different groups that went to separate worksites each day. Each night we returned to camp to hear amazing stories of groups sharing the gospel with the owners of the homes on their worksites; we had yet to meet the lady that lived at ours. Several of the students in my group expressed their sadness and frustration as the week neared its ending and we still hadn't met Betsy. Part of the discussion I had with them included this: sharing the gospel is not always about having a direct conversation with someone. Sometimes it looks more like "being" the gospel. We never got to see her reaction, but I am sure when Betsy returned home to see her french drain, she felt loved and valued. She had interacted with the youth workers from the organization that worked with us that week, and I know they made it clear that we were there because of our love for her that we had because of our love for Jesus. We don't always see the results of our sharing/being the gospel. Maybe we will when we get to heaven one day, but until then, we trust that God is at work.

While reading my goal journal after the trip, I turned to a page that said, "go on another mission trip." I wrote that entry the year I graduated high school, after my first mission trip, which was exactly ten years prior. What a cool thing to look back on that page and see that God knows our heart's desire and sees even the seemingly small things.

The few weeks left of summer were spent preparing my classroom and getting ready to meet my students. I received my class list and had to chuckle at God, again knowing me and my thoughts. Several students had moved to other schools from an already small 2nd grade group, so my roster consisted of twelve students. In my district, the typical bilingual classroom is anywhere from 18–26. A class size of twelve is unheard of; yet, God gave me that opportunity to have a somewhat small group and honor my willingness to move forward with something I wasn't quite comfortable with.

The fall semester was fantastic. I had worked with every single one of my students during the previous two years, so I knew them fairly well, and we were quickly becoming a family. We learned each other's strengths and struggles as we practiced reading and math and learned what it meant to be a good friend, sibling, son/daughter, and student. My students were making outstanding growth academically and continued to impress me with their social interactions.

One silly thing I was looking forward to as a classroom teacher was the Christmas gifts—seems so shallow, I know. Not that I expected anything grandiose, but as a resource teacher (pulling out small groups of students), I didn't really get many gifts from my students. Hear me out: it ultimately doesn't matter, but it feels good to be appreciated! That being said, before I was a classroom teacher, I had received a lifetime supply of kind words, cute pictures, cards, and coloring book pages that still sit in a "cheer up" file in my basement.

Despite my desire for cheap Christmas gifts, delivered with love, God had other plans. The Thursday before break, I had some neck pain. After dinner, I told Chris I wasn't feeling well and went to bed early. My sleep was fitful and sparse. Waking up to throw up is one of the worst things. If you know, you know. I mean, let's be real. I don't think throwing up is EVER an enjoyable experience, but when it happens in the dark, on the floor next to your bed, into your plastic garbage can—it's at the top of the list of "things I hope I never have to do." It happened more than once that night. By the time I decided I wouldn't be able to go to work that Friday, I was dehydrated, my neck hurt, and a brass band was trying to escape from my skull.

You know what teachers do when they are sick? They write sub plans. So, there I was, half sitting up in bed, trying to write about all of the fun activities I had planned for my kiddos that day. It was the last Friday before Christmas break, and I was sad to miss it. Around 6:30, I hit submit on the too-bright screen as I slid my computer onto my night stand and gently lowered myself onto my pillows. By this point, the pressure in my head was almost intolerable. That, by itself, should have been enough to wave the white flag of surrender and let my husband drive me to the hospital, but I was convinced I didn't need to go. He was pretty sure I did.

For almost eight more hours, I drifted in and out of sleep (or consciousness, I'm not honestly sure). Of course, my husband was checking on me throughout the day. He wasn't able to convince me that the situation warranted an ER visit, so he called my parents, his parents, my siblings-anyone that could join his side of the argument. By 2:00 pm it wasn't up to me anymore. I was barely responsive, and he couldn't get me out of bed.

"We are going to the hospital right now." I remember his worried words.

The next thing I knew, there was a rush of cold air coming from the front door as the EMTs hurried into our bedroom and loaded me onto a stretcher. I wasn't aware of much, but unfortunately, I remember the look of despair on Chris' face. I should've listened to his eight hours of pleading. I should've let him take me.

I laid on the emergency room bed, curled into a fetal position as they did a lumbar puncture and tears slid down my cheeks. When I awoke and asked for Chris, they wouldn't let me see him. Back into the fitful sleep I went. The next time I opened my eyes, he was there and I was in the ICU. Chris gently responded to my disbelief at how fast they had moved me into the ICU by explaining that I had actually been in the ER for nearly eight hours. I didn't remember anything except the lumbar puncture.

Sepsis.

It's a scary word, and I didn't really know exactly what it meant until the next day. Thankfully, my body was somewhat responsive to the attack, and I was coming out of the fog. I learned that I had been septic and that I indeed did have meningitis. I laid there in disbelief as Chris told me through tear-filled eyes that he hadn't been sure that I was going to make it through the night.

At that point, I didn't truly come to grips with how dire the situation had presented itself. After a day and a half, the nurses moved me out of the ICU. I thanked nurse Shelley for her kindness and gentleness. She had been with me almost twenty four of the hours I had been in the ICU through two of her twelve-hour shifts and I was grateful for her care. Shelley assured me that the nurses on the floor would be better than her and that it would benefit me to get into a quieter space.

She was right that it was quiet. I'm not sure if it benefitted me though! I was recovering quicker than expected, but they weren't about to let me walk away after what my body had experienced. Plus, I hadn't had a bowel movement yet. So, I watched a lot of HGTV and probably some Christmas movies, as the holiday was only nine days away. Chris was able to spend most nights with me, but after the initial three days, he needed a break (who can blame him?). He also had to go back to work.

Let me throw in a quick tribute to caregivers, parents, and/ or spouses of those with chronic illnesses. My husband has been amazing through every single one of these experiences. Yes, his anxiety has risen quite a bit, and the gray patch of hair behind his ear may be my fault, but he has walked faithfully by my side despite the concern, worry, and fear that can come with the unknown of having a chronically sick loved one. As the person who was sick, I've always felt like I didn't really have a choice. I was stuck in the hospital bed, so I had to stay positive in order to recover the fastest. As the person watching a loved one go through all of that garbage, your choices are different. I can imagine that it is difficult. Chris has shared some of his feelings of helplessness and sorrow, but I'm sure his fear ran deep as he watched me lay unconscious in that ICU bed, prayed in the waiting room as I endured a four-hour brain surgery, and stood by as I wasn't acting like myself while on morphine after the surgery. Plus, the concern that bubbles up every time I say I have neck pain, wondering if this time it will send us back to the hospital. I am grateful for his resilience and his ability to make the hard choices. Plus, he knows when to call in replacements or when to ask for advice. I don't think this is what he quite had in mind as he repeated "in sickness and in health" during our wedding vows, but he has never stopped loving me. I will forever love and admire him for all of these things.

Some of my family was able to visit from Green Bay, which was nice, but when no one was there, it was as quiet as nurse Shelley had mentioned, and it wasn't just for lack of action.

My ear had started to bother me almost immediately after leaving the ICU. One of my nurses brought q-tips, and we tried hydrogen peroxide, but nothing seemed to help. It felt like it was full of earwax, but there was little to be found.

Real quick story about another time in my life when helpful people were sticking q-tips in my orifices. When I was three or four, I continued to complain about the tag on my shirt while we were on an airplane. One of my parents had ripped it off and for some reason, let me have it. Next thing they knew, I was crying because I had shoved it so far up my nose that I couldn't get it out. I'm not sure what my thought process was at that point, but I'm sure I just wanted to rid myself of the dumb tag. Since we were thousands of feet in the air, we were left with no choice but to rely on the flight attendants. Someone had q-tips to spare, and after several minutes, they pried that tag out of my nose like they were digging for gold. I'm sure the whole plane breathed a sigh of relief!

As I mentioned, trying to use the cotton-swabbed sticks in the hospital was much less successful. The discomfort only got worse over the next couple of days. Despite that, everything else seemed to be improving and moving. The culture they had taken of my spinal fluid in the ER grew bacteria. So, unlike all of my previous diagnoses of meningitis, they were able to determine that it was bacterial meningitis this time, and they knew it was caused by strep B. They were discharging me after five days and sending me home on self-administered antibiotics.

Although it took awhile to have a bowel movement at the hospital, my body had no issue producing a multitude of waste once I got home. The next several days, I had terrible diarrhea and nausea. The doctor prescribed me Zofran to no avail. I couldn't keep anything down; I was losing strength, and spending most of my time throwing up, waiting to throw up, or pooping. With concern, the doc told me to come in to get tested for C. diff, which is a bacterial infection that can start after starting antibiotics.

Back to the hospital we went, and although I walked out on my own two feet just a few days before that–I could barely hold myself up at that point. I was angry that none of these symptoms had happened while I was still under the watchful eyes and caring hands of the nurses. I had no problem giving them the sample they needed for the test, although Chris did have to guide me to the bathroom. The results came by phone that afternoon, and surprisingly, there was no secondary infection.

After another call to the doctor, we realized that I had been administering the antibiotic too quickly due to an explanation error made by my discharge nurse. This was causing the miserable trifecta of diarrhea, nausea, and vomit. All of my symptoms subsided after twenty four hours of correctly taking the antibiotics. If you're keeping track, it was Christmas Eve eve at this point.

Our fam came for a whirlwind visit consisting of a barrage of colorful wrapping paper, thank yous, and well wishes. Of course they wished they could stay but didn't want to impose, so after the gift opening, they were on their way home, despite my insisting that they stay. I was able to stay prone for the first time in over a week, so we did the only logical thing: made a gingerbread house.

Christmas and New Years came and went with less than the usual excitement. No fancy dresses or champagne. We laid low and thanked the Lord that we weren't still in the hospital.

The first few weeks of 2017 weren't much to read about, so I'll gloss right over the multitude of doctor visits. About the fourth week in though, I went to the audiologist. My ear had not gotten better, which was unusual and concerning. I explained to her what the last six weeks had looked like for me and gave details of the bout of meningitis. The look of concern appeared on her face almost immediately. Dr. Oreja offered a simple sentence that I wasn't expecting: meningitis can sometimes cause permanent hearing loss.

Had I heard her correctly? Pun unintended, and not humorous at the time, as I questioned it in my thoughts. Hearing loss? After going through what I just went through? It didn't really seem fair, let alone likely. I asked her the next steps and how she could know if the damage was permanent or if maybe I did just have some earwax.

Into the little soundbooth I went, after Dr. Oreja handed me the headphones. As the pings and tings and bells sounded in my right ear, I didn't hear them as often in my left. I tried to raise my hand only when I heard the sound, but the weird thing about hearing tests is that sometimes you want so badly to hear the sound that you think you actually do. Does this only happen to me? I'm sure not! I can studiously and calmly sit through any standardized academic test, but put me in a soundbooth and tell me to raise my hand when I hear a sound, and I get nervous that I'm going to do it wrong. Please tell me it's not just me.

Within a week, I returned for my results. Dr. O showed me the metrics and confirmed that I had hearing loss. She hypothesized it was indeed from meningitis and that it most likely would be permanent. I held on to the slim chance that she said existed for my eardrum to heal and return to its previous functioning. I had lost over 60% of my hearing. My body had truly been through the wringer.

Of course, by that point, I had already struggled with how close to death I had actually been. Life felt different. I don't really know how to put it into words, but realizing that you could have died had the circumstances gone just slightly differently, changes your outlook a bit. Little things that may have bothered me in the past, didn't anymore. The fact that I couldn't hear much out of my left ear barely registered, considering I was healthy otherwise. It was humbling and invigorating at the same time.

This reaction was much more optimistic than the first time I had this realization after my brain surgery. Post surgery, I suddenly felt more mortal than ever. Fears that didn't exist before surgery suddenly crept into my psyche. I couldn't believe that I had once traveled over two miles in an underground cave and traversed spaces that were only slightly bigger than my body. The fact that I had jumped off of a thirty-foot waterfall was close to paralyzing when I even thought about considering doing it again. I wasn't untouchable anymore, and my zipper scar was proof of that.

Hear me when I say that I am now thankful for that scar. It is proof that I am a fighter and that I have a powerful God on my side. It is evidence of a courageous step of faith to let another human take my life into his hands and come out on the other side. It is a mark of hardwork and healing after years of hurt. Yes, I am thankful for the scar, but it definitely changed my level of bravery.

I had been working in elementary schools for the past five years and loving (almost) every second of it. When the meningitis came again, it was time for a change. As I'm sure most of you know, children aren't the best at keeping their germs to themselves. To this day, I have a vivid memory of one of my students sneezing directly into my face and then being in the hospital a couple days later with a swollen brain. That being said, I didn't want to leave education, but I wasn't sure what that could look like or what my options were.

It was literally about a week after I had started praying for a new job that my district emailed us about a position they were creating for the following year: content area facilitator. Essentially, the role involved coaching and working with teachers across the district with a specific content area. It was literally an answer to prayer. I would be able to stay in my district, continue working with teachers and students (just a little bit further away), and share all of the wonderful strategies and ideas I had learned over the years. I completed the interview (which involved a fun presentation on how to make paper airplanes) and was offered the position of Science and Social Science Facilitator the same day.

Miracles

One thing you should know about miracles, is that they still happen. I haven't been privy to any literal partings of seas lately, but I have seen plenty of "yay Gods." If you look for them, they're all around—especially the small ones. The big ones don't happen as often, and when they do, some people try to explain them away. Most of the time though, they can't. Not really. God likes doing miracles that can ONLY be attributed to Him. The fact that I went into remission *two years* after my doctor had ever seen anyone go into remission can really only be explained by a God-sized miracle.

I believe He puts us in circumstances from which He is the only one who can save us. Think Shadrach, Meshach, and Abednego in the fiery furnace (Daniel 3, ESV), Daniel in the lion's den (Daniel 6, ESV), Israelites crossing the Red Sea (Exodus 14, ESV), David and Goliath (1 Samuel 17, NLT), cancer diagnoses, kidney disease, failing marriages, lost children, etc. Whatever your mountain is, God is bigger than it!

Notice the miracles and then tell people about them. Be a miracle reporter.

Moment for Reflection

Have you witnessed any miracles lately? In the past? Write about them here.

_____

_____

_____

_____

_____

_____

_____

14

Baby?

The job wasn't great.

Our district hadn't really prepared for what our jobs might look like, and honestly, teachers weren't really sure what to expect. They felt like we were spying on them whenever we came into their classrooms, they didn't like it when we attended their team meetings, and we struggled to get more than a handful of people to come to our *optional* professional development sessions.

Disappointed, and unsure of how to make the most of my days holed up (not by choice) in my office, I started a science blog. I loved researching unique animals and scientific phenomena and writing about them in a way that would make sense to kids! I spent the rest of my time creating projects and lesson supports that hardly got used with students. Our elementary teachers had struggled for years to "find the time" to teach science (gasp and shed a tear), and by not allowing me to require teacher attendance or implementation, I didn't have much buy-in. I sought out the teachers who I knew were willing to try new things and spent time in their classrooms working with students who were loving "doing science."

The school year wore me out. For the first time, I was considering a career outside of education. I wouldn't really call what I experienced "burn out," but it was dreadful all the same. For a passionate, lifelong learner, who loves facilitating learning, to consider a job other than as an educator, it was a heartbreaking spring semester. I toyed with the idea of working at our local community college teaching adult ESL, but never really pursued it. My next great idea was to rent a little storefront in our neighborhood that had just been listed for sale and open a brick and mortar creative shop. I was dreaming of curating art from local artisans and makers and selling it. The dream also included hosting sign making and faux calligraphy classes for those interested in honing their creative skills in a cozy maker space.

The rent was practically as much as our mortgage, so we tabled the idea. Chris and I prayed about the future and a few weeks later, got what seemed to be an answer. District leadership was changing and they were revamping my position. I would have to re-apply, which was annoying, but not the end of the world. They were also adding a specialist in the area of Language Learners, so my intrigue and passion in that area inspired me to stay.

The interview was the most interesting one I've ever participated in. All of the content coordinators, there were six of them, sat around the north end of the table, while I sat on the south end. Each round of questioning left me feeling more prepared for the position and more excited about the prospect. The last question was unexpected though. One of the coordinators asked me which content area I would prefer. I guess the question itself wasn't that unexpected, of course they wanted to know that, but the response to my answer was what left me feeling awkward. I responded that I would happily work in any of the content areas, but that Language Learners have a special place in my heart. As I explained that working as the Language Learner specialist would allow me to support all content areas, the science coordinator jumped in with, "I would love to have you work with science." Practically interrupting her, the language learner coordinator expressed her interest in working with me and a couple of the other coordinators ditto'd her sentiments.

Later that afternoon, I was officially asked which role I would choose. After some deliberation, I chose the language learner position and thanked Jesus for this role that it seemed I had been preparing for my entire career. I would get to work with bilingual teachers to support their growth as well as their students' growth. I left for summer break with a renewed vigor and positive outlook.

I haven't mentioned yet, that during the fall of 2016 and spring of 2017, I was attending the last few courses for my Masters in Educational Leadership and writing my thesis. Due to the meningitis the previous December, I didn't get as much thesis writing completed as I had hoped, so I was actively working on it during 2017. I was thrilled to share my findings that despite the MAP assessment (standardized test in Illinois) not being normed for language learners, and being an English assessment, my bilingual third graders had outperformed their monolingual peers on both reading and math. It was such a testament to their hard work!

On a snowy day in December of 2017, Chris and I drove to Kenosha for my thesis defense. Although we were required to pose an invitation to the entire campus, my three professors were the only ones who attended (might have had something to do with it being on a Friday night). Anyway, I was grateful to not have to present to a room full of people I hardly knew. Since I was completing my graduate work years after I had attended the same college full-time, I didn't really have any relational ties to the school except for those three professors.

It needs to be said that I am so appreciative of the time and energy those mentors poured into my project. Dr. Z reminded me of the significance that my thesis had from a historical perspective on education in the United States and supported me with a happy heart. Profe M had been my mentor for almost ten years at that point, and I was grateful for his continual support, encouragement, and guidance. He had helped me create the most amazing study abroad experience, walked me through my undergraduate thesis, and met with me several times to tweak my graduate thesis. Dr. Q was responsible for most of my quantitative work and really developed my appreciation for numbers that had started when I was young, but had truly flourished into a well-researched, and fully supportable, quantitative project.

The presentation went off without a hitch, and I had successfully defended my thesis. They encouraged me to turn it into a paper and submit it to a few educational journals, but unfortunately, I never took the time. I was happy to be finished and received my diploma a couple of weeks later. With the diploma, came a few bound copies of my thesis. It was technically the first book I had ever "published," and it felt good to hold it in my hands. It has always been a dream of mine to write a book, and although it didn't really count, I still relished in the accomplishment.

That same month, I found myself doubting God.

Chris and I had finally made the decision to move forward with an adoption. In September, we attended an informational meeting held by an adoption agency that had been recommended to us by some friends. The meeting was a bit overwhelming as they explained the many options for adding a baby to our family through adoption. The most overwhelming thing about it was that it would cost between $30-$45,000! We didn't have that kind of money laying around, especially after I had just borrowed another student loan to finish my Masters. Like I said, I was doubting God. He had put this desire to adopt in our hearts, but I didn't see how it could possibly happen.

He's the God of the universe, people. He's performed unbelievable, incredible, awesome miracles for thousands of years (not to mention His creation of all that we know), and I didn't think He could find this amount of money for us to bring home one of His children. After thinking this way for a few months, I had an epiphany/realization/moment of clarity (whatever you want to call it) while driving to work. I immediately repented of my disbelief and prayed fervently that He would make it possible if it really was what He wanted us to do. I had been praying previously for this, but somehow, in my human brain, I couldn't imagine how it could actually happen.

Also during this time, Chris and I were both feeling like we needed to be able to rely on our family and friends in order for this process to be successful. We are pretty independent people and definitely struggle to ask for help and/or receive that help. So, we were also praying for God to give us the courage to rely on others.

Are you ready for this next part?!

God answers prayers you guys!

It had been about three weeks since I had asked for forgiveness for doubting God, and we still hadn't seen any flashing lights nor had we won the lottery, so we decided that maybe we should take a step of faith and ask for help through a fundraising page. Afterall, someone had recently crowdfunded tens of thousands of dollars for potato salad, so I'm sure we could accomplish our more honorable goal. We wrote our story, set up a page, and shared with our parents and siblings that it would be live the next day. After speaking with Chris' mom, she asked that we not make it live yet and said that she would call us later. Of course, we were confused, but we waited. A couple hours later, we heard back from her.

God had provided the money through family members that offered to fund our adoption. Insert BIG alligator tears. Moral of this story: pray big prayers and believe that God will answer them, because He will!

Ask and it will be given to you;

seek and you will find;

knock and the door will be opened to you.

Matthew 7:7
NIV

Pray Big Prayers

In Matthew chapter 7, Jesus tells us to, "Ask and it will be given to you; seek and you will find; knock and the door will be opened to you."

Sometimes praying big prayers is scary. Taking even the smallest step of faith can feel like an insurmountable challenge, but it is that very thing which allows God to do His best work. Now, don't get me wrong, God is doing work whether we give Him the space to or not, but when we decide to put our full trust in Him, it allows us to recognize His good work. Sometimes what He is doing goes unnoticed because we are too caught up in our fear and our doubts to recognize it.

Moment for Reflection

If you are feeling trapped, scared, overwhelmed, or unsure about your next step, I encourage you to have a conversation with the Lord. Explain to Him how you're feeling and then acknowledge His Lordship over your life. Offer those feelings over to Him and prepare yourself to walk lighter, taller, and happier in the freedom of His provision. He cares for His children and wants a relationship with them. He is worthy of our praise. He wants it; so, give it to Him.

15

Meeting the Others

Rare is a good thing when it comes to gemstones or collector's items, but rare can also be isolating, intimidating, and scary when it comes to a disease or diagnosis. For the first thirty one years of my life, including eight years post-diagnosis, I hadn't met anyone in person that had the same disease as me. That all changed the summer of 2018. The Lymphangiomatosis and Gorham's Disease Alliance (LGDA) was hosting their second Patient and Family Conference in Texas, and Chris and I decided to attend.

A little background on the LGDA. It is a nonprofit organization that's purpose is "patient support, education, and outreach; supporting scientific and clinical research; and building partnerships that advance the mission (lgdalliance.org)." It was started by Jana K. Sheets, a patient, in 2007. Currently, it is run by a board of directors (now led by Dr. K!) as well as many volunteers. I'm grateful for the help they provided in finding Dr. K, as well as their continued advocacy work.

We flew down to Grapevine, TX with positive anxiety. You know, the kind of emotion that has you giddy and sweating at the same time (or maybe that was just the Texas heat?). I had been grateful for the virtual connections made with other fighters online, but nothing beats face-to-face conversation. At the meet-and-greet that first evening, we swapped stories and shared our scars. Having the same rare disease immediately formed a bond between us. To stand in the same room as others who have gone through what you have is surreal. We had endured the same weird symptoms, dealt with the annoying blank looks from doctors, experienced all the emotions about whether or not to have surgery, and had an internal debate about how to talk about our disease with friends and coworkers. It's hard to put into words, but the experience was simply priceless.

The conference was phenomenal. We listened to world-class researchers and experts who knew everything there was to know about our particular diseases. That wasn't a lot of information, but it was more than we had heard up to this point. One of the sessions included a Q&A with a panel of all of the doctors that attended the conference, and it was such an amazing opportunity to pick the brains of these specialists after so many years of trying to explain what little I knew of my disease to any doctor I saw. There were only about thirty patients there (each with family members and caretakers), so we had elite access to the doctors.

Chris and I chatted with several of them after each of their presentations, and we were able to gain insight into the intricacies of the disease. For someone with two rare diseases, who often knew more than her treating physician, I felt like I couldn't keep up with the flow of information. I learned that there were children in Spain with my disease that had meningitis every other month (so my measly four, maybe five, cases in my thirty years didn't seem like much to the Spanish doctor). One of the researchers presented his findings that hadn't even been shared in a paper yet and let us in on the ground floor of the possibility of knowing a genetic marker for our disease. This was astonishing news! It opened up the possibility of diagnosing the disease from birth (or earlier) and studying the disease process much earlier than they had been able to. Near the end of the conference, he was presented with an award for this groundbreaking research.

> Share your celebrations and struggles related to your disease with others who will understand. It is helpful to be in community with those who face a similar situation.

The purpose of this story isn't for you, as the reader, to become an expert in GLA or Gorham's Stout Disease, because most of you have your own thing for which you are responsible for educating others on, but I do want to give you somewhat of a look into the disease process. It gets a little complicated, so bear with me.

Essentially, there are three types of lymphatic, or vascular, anomalies that are associated with lymphangiomatosis. Each type has a similar underlying disease process that involves abnormally interconnected and dilated cysts in the lymphatic system (which is an intricate system that is present all over your body). The differences between the types of the disease are where those cysts are located. Lymphangiomatosis, now called GLA, or generalized lymphatic anomaly, is when these cysts are present in soft tissue like organs (and is sometimes used as a blanket diagnosis or term). Gorham's Stout disease (also known as disappearing bone disease) is the presence of the lymphatic cysts in bone, hence the nickname. The last type of the disease is KLA, or kaposiform lymphangiomatosis, which affects the lungs.

As far as they know, the lymphatic system is affected when the fetus is in utero. Extra pockets of lymph are created that aren't correctly connected to the rest of the system. These lymph cysts can swell and cause a lot of damage to the surrounding tissue and/or bone. When my GLA was diagnosed, it was found mostly in my spine and skull and had caused lesions or holes in many of the bones in that area, appearing like swiss cheese (granting me the weird Dr. Seuss comments from the pathologist). Now that they know more specifics about the disease, I know I have Gorham's Stout and GLA since the disease involvement is mostly in my bones but also in some of my soft tissue.

Much of this delineation has come from recent (in the last ten years and since my diagnosis) research. It is fascinating, yet frustrating, to have a disease that even the leading lymph experts know very little about, but I am grateful for those who are passionate about learning more about lymphatic anomalies and trying to find effective treatments and possibly a cure. During the conference, we also learned that doctors who choose to go into research, especially for rare diseases that have little mainstream attention, must fundraise their own salaries and financial support for projects. Many of the doctors at the conference worked at research hospitals, but were not paid by those facilities. Therefore, when you see fundraising events for rare diseases, know that your generous donation is going directly to funding research and supporting the committed doctors who conduct that research.

I discovered that I was the only person at the conference who wasn't currently being treated for my symptoms. To be fair, I was taking pain medication as needed, but comparatively, that was pretty tame. Most of the others were on one or the other immunosuppressive drug in hopes to shrink their cysts and minimize the long-term effects of the disease. Thankfully, the lymph pockets in my body were fairly stable. I was still dealing with at-least-weekly migraines and lots of somehow-caused neck pain, but was grateful I hadn't needed to start a difficult treatment option that would make me vulnerable to even more infections. Day-to-day, the GLA and Gorham's were impacting me in other ways, such as not being able to fully work out, get too hot, or do any repetitive motion. When watching TV or movies, I had to switch positions a few times to ensure that my neck wasn't twisted a certain way for too long. During the summer, the air conditioning was my best friend, and in order to garden or do yard work, I purchased a cooling towel to wear around my neck.

Annoying, to be sure, but I've learned how to manage the triggers as best as possible, and I wake up every morning grateful for the healing I've experienced.

We left the conference appreciating a newly energized support network and headed a little further south to visit my dad and stepmom for a few days. It was a fun visit, and I enjoyed decompressing from the conference and discussing all of the information with them. They both work in the medical field and were fascinated to hear about the new findings. We chatted over delicious tex-mex food, visited The Alamo (so much fascinating history tied to that place), and admired the cityscape and people watching along the bustling San Antonio Riverwalk. What a cool city!

Heading home after the conference, our focus returned to our desire to grow our family. The agency we decided to work with only maintains a certain number of couples on their waitlist, and since their adoption placements were down that year, they were not running any classes until at least spring of 2019. Disappointed, yet hopeful for what was to come, we waited for March.

Chris and I truly enjoyed the classes and learned a lot. We attended with several other couples who were joining the list of "people who can't wait to grow their family" and it was again nice to be in a room where you knew your emotions were met with similar ones in the hearts and minds of the attendees. Our situation was slightly different than most though, since we hadn't had to deal with infertility, as many of them had.

Not only were we able to share with others on the adoption journey, but we also got to hear from both a birth mother as well as an adoptive mother who had already gone through it. The stories that were shared that weekend were perspective-giving and eye-opening. It helped to hear about adoption from other angles and realize that there is a lot of loss and pain in the adoption triad (which consists of: birth parents, adoptive parents, and adopted child). We explored even further than that to extended family members on both sides of the adoption. I hadn't thought about the birth grandparents until that day, and it made me pause and reflect on the whole thing. For those who aren't familiar, there is a lot of potential for hurt and loss in adoption, and often those feelings and emotions are experienced, but there is also the potential for great joy.

But if anyone has the world's goods & sees his brother IN NEED, yet closes his heart against him how does God's love abide in him?

1 John 3:17
ESV

Invisible

In order to raise awareness, after the conference, the LGDA had asked those affected by these diseases to share their stories. With this book already started, I knew my story was more than the 500 2000 words requested, so I chose to write a poem instead. If you are interested, you can read it here: https://www.lgdalliance.org/amber/. Check out the stories from the other fighters as well, if you get a chance!

Please remember that you never know what someone might be going through. This particular disease is invisible to those around us, but we live with the symptoms every day. There are many diseases that don't have external or visible symptoms. Rare diseases affect nearly one in ten Americans, which means that there are more people in the U.S. living with rare diseases than cancer and stroke/ heart attack patients combined. That is not to diminish what folks living with either of those are going through, but only to say that we know a lot more and hear about the effects of cancer and heart attacks much more often than we hear about rare diseases.

Extend grace, show kindness, and be a friend to those you meet. You never know what someone is going through.

Moment for Reflection

Do you know anyone with a rare disease? If so, purpose to learn more about it. Either ask that person to share their story or spend some time researching. If you don't know anyone with a rare disease, choose a random one. You can start at rarediseases.org.
Rare disease to research:

_____

_____

_____

_____

16

Still Waiting

This chapter will be a little different than the rest. Chris and I have been keeping a blog throughout the adoption, and I wanted to share some of those words with you to give you a glimpse into what we were feeling in the moment through this firsthand narrative.

Drug Testing and Other Drudgery
Author: Chris
May 19, 2019

During the process to get our home study started, one of the requirements was a sort of physical wellness evaluation to be filled out by our doctors. When I initially went, I realized I needed a TB test, along with the other routine things you do during a physical. A couple days later I picked up the form and sent it to the adoption agency. I was then reminded that I had missed a urine drug testing panel that had to be completed and filled out.

So I went back to the doctor's office and as best that I can recall – I think this was the first time in my adult life I have been asked to pee in a cup. I haven't moved jobs or been part of any criminal proceedings in recent years (or ever), so there has been no need for a drug test.

I entered the lab and was handed a cup with an unbroken seal – good start. In the bathroom, I scoffed as I saw instructions on the wall for how to give a urine sample. "Why would anyone need instructions on how to pee into something?" After all, being a male, I've been peeing into things for a while now. Back in college when any of us woke up in the middle of the night, we would just find an empty Gatorade bottle to pee in instead of walking out into the blinding light of the hallway that led to the urinal.

I scoffed again as I read the instructions closely – to paraphrase, they said to begin peeing into the toilet, move the cup so that you are now peeing into the cup, then as the cup fills, move it again to finish peeing into the toilet. I thought it'd be a recipe for disaster if one were to move the cup mid-stream. It would get all over the outside of the cup, and I could only imagine the horror of having to hand the lab worker a wet cup.

Needless to say, I did not follow the directions and I just peed directly into the cup because it seemed pretty silly that they needed instructions for such a simple thing. Pleasantly surprised by my hydrated-ness, I carefully closed the container and handed it off to the lab.

It didn't occur to me until later that the instructions probably assumed you would stop peeing before moving the cup. Amber had to remind me of that. She also told me that they put the instructions up because that method allows for a clean sample of urine. Unless my boxers were lined with drugs I think I'll be ok.

If you just read all of that and thought, "That's a bit much in the way of personal information," I've gotta say, that's about how we felt as we finished filling out all the paperwork to get our home study started. We had many forms to fill out, some with more questions than articles of ill-fitting clothes in my closet. Not all the questions were easy to answer either. Some of the easier questions that stood out were everyday, normal things you think about on a regular basis, like "How do you plan to discipline your child?", "What are the ages of the people living in your neighborhood?", and "Will your child have access to multicultural role models if they sought them out?"

If you couldn't tell, I'm being facetious. Those are not things I think about on a regular basis – does anyone?

I'm happy to say my drug test came back negative—which allows us to officially say our initial home study paperwork has been completed and submitted. More to come with updates as we go through our home study.

What Kind of Underwear Do You Have On?

Authors: Amber & Chris
May 25, 2019

When you think "home study," you probably think of a social worker scouring sock drawers for hidden vices, counting up the number of knives and guns, and noting the numerous unsafe areas for a child to get into trouble.

Thankfully, that hasn't happened–yet. Last week, we initiated our home study with a two-hour office visit with our very sweet social worker. The visit was fairly benign, yet felt like talking to a stranger about what kind of underwear you have on. As we drove to the office, Chris mentioned he was a bit nervous. I acknowledged his nerves, but reminded him that we are who we are. There's no studying or practicing for a home study. Trying to come up with canned responses or hoping to say what they want to hear is like putting lipstick on a pig. Not to say we live in a pen, or even that we walk around in mud all day, or can't offer what they are looking for. It's more like–you get what you get. Ultimately, God's in control.

Now, I do completely understand the nerves. I mean, it's weird having to talk to someone we've known for barely three months about our hopes and dreams, fears and struggles, and how we plan to raise our child. The questions were deeply personal. Like, the dark part of the ocean deep. Despite all the emotions, it is super beneficial to think through these things and reflect as a couple on some really important questions. Our responses have left me feeling confident that Chris and I are on the same page about most of the important stuff and gave me a peek into the future of us as parents. It's exciting dreaming together and talking through some of these things–it's just strange having to do it in front of someone else. I don't want you to get the impression that we felt pressured or uncomfortable, because thankfully, our social worker did a great job of helping us feel at ease, it's still just weird. Back to the underwear metaphor–I'm sure you have no problem talking to your significant other about it, but now imagine someone else being in the room.

That was just the first step in the process, and it wasn't even in our home. Next, we have to take an online survey (individually) that will ask us even more questions. Boxers or briefs? Etc … From there, we each meet with our social worker individually to dig through our childhood.

The last step in the process is more like what you envision when you hear "home study." She will spend several hours (upwards of four to five) in our home. I'm sure we will have plenty to share about that when the time comes. Until then, consider discussing your underclothes with your significant other–just do it somewhere where it's just the two of you.

Stamp of Approval
Authors: Amber & Chris
July 1, 2019

It's been ten days.

Ten days since we heard those long-awaited words.

We sat across from our social worker in our living room on a sunny summer afternoon. She discussed the results of the two hundred question assessment we took and explained that we were a "vitalized" couple. Part of the explanation included a debrief on twelve relationship categories and how we could manage life pretty well as a couple (it's great to hear, even after–especially after–seven years of marriage) The next hour we reviewed our preferences (for the fourth time), which is still such a weird thing. We have to decide what we are comfortable with and what we don't necessarily feel equipped to handle. I mean, everything from what drugs the birth mom took during pregnancy (like, cocaine vs. marijuana, etc.), to her family's medical and mental history, to if we want her to have a part in naming the baby. I mean, these are *very* important decisions, but at the same time, it's like, why/how am I even deciding what I'm okay with? Thankfully, we know that God already knows our baby and knows exactly the circumstances that sweet baby will come from. We just need to abide in His provision and perfect timing. Easier said than done.

After we discussed several potentially life-altering questions, we guided our SW around the house in a quick tour. Essentially, she wanted to know that we weren't hoarders. In all seriousness though, the tour was short and just enough to show her that we have ample space to welcome a child into our home.

The quick tour was over, and she informed us happily, "you are approved." Chris and I high fived each other as our SW smiled. Now, we are waiting to hear the next three words: "you are matched."

Until then, we still have time to cover all the outlets and relocate our cleaning supplies to higher ground.

Wait for It
Author: Amber & Chris
July 29, 2019

Three hundred thirty two days have passed since we submitted our adoption application.

We completed thirty six hours of training.

We answered upwards of *one thousand* personal questions about ourselves, our spouse, and our families.

We gave urine samples, had blood drawn, and were proven physically fit.

We wrote and printed thirteen profile books (the agency only needed eight, but Office Max was on the struggle bus).

We prayed. A lot.

We crossed the t's and dotted the i's, and we are finally a "waiting family."

And now–we wait, and pray. Of course, there are still so many things to do, including securing a lawyer, completing a CPR class, decorating a nursery, and finishing our registry. We are now at the point where we have done what we needed to do. The rest is in God's hands. Ironically, He has been reminding us just exactly what that means for Chris and I and what it has meant for so many others.

He has been teaching us so much throughout this process, and I am so grateful for His provision and gentle reminders. Let me give you a glimpse into the multitude of God's goodness!

In June, I taught the story of Moses and the ten plagues (Exodus) during Vacation Bible School. Through preparation time, and during my lessons that week, I reflected on Moses's story of *adoption*, and how that was part of God's plan to redeem His people from Egypt. At the time Moses was born, Pharaoh had ordered that all the male Hebrew babies be thrown into the Nile River. Moses's mom knew this and wanted to protect her son, so she hid him for three months. When she could no longer hide him, she sent him down the Nile in a basket. By the grace of God, Pharaoh's daughter found baby Moses and chose to raise him as her own. When she needed a midwife, Moses's sister (who had followed his basket down the Nile) suggested she run to get a Hebrew woman. Of course, she chose her own mother (who was also Moses's mom, if you're following) who then nursed Moses and cared for him until the time came to bring him back to Pharaoh's daughter. Moses was then raised as a prince of Egypt in Pharaoh's kingdom. The story continues as God calls

Moses and uses his obedience to save His people out of the bondage of slavery.

God used adoption to save an entire nation of His people! Wow! The graciousness, strength, love, and humility that Moses's birth mom possessed, allowed her to provide a safe life for him. What an awesome example of how birth moms are trying to do what is best for their children! I am grateful for the decision our child's birth mom will make and that we will be blessed by her sacrificial willingness to trust us to raise her child. God is good.

In my women's Bible study this summer, we have been spending a lot of time in the old testament with powerful, God-fearing women like Leah, Hannah, and Sarah. Here is a brief synopsis of each of their stories:

Leah - she was given to her husband Jacob as a trick and therefore felt very unloved. God saw her pain and opened her womb so that she was able to have many sons. Her sister Rachel (who was truly loved by their husband Jacob) tormented her. God used Leah's story to show us that He sees our struggle, knows us, and wants us to focus on Him. Leah bore sons until she praised God for them. God wanted her (and wants us) to find her (our) peace and rest in Him alone— not in the love of a man, in babies, or in any other worldly desire.

Hannah - she was barren and because of this, was ridiculed consistently by her husband's other wife (yes, lots of sin in the Bible). Every year, when the family went to the synagogue, Hannah cried out to the Lord, "O Lord of hosts, if you will indeed look on the affliction of your servant and remember me and not forget your servant, but will give to your servant a son, then I will give him to the Lord all the days of his life, and no razor shall touch his head." (1 Samuel 1:10–13, ESV) It says later in 1 Samuel, that the Lord remembered Hannah and she conceived in due time. Again, the Lord saw the anguish of His child and gave her the desire of her heart because she knew that only God could provide. In return, Hannah dedicated her son to the Lord.

Sarah (Sarai) - she was the wife of Abraham (Abram) and was also barren. She took matters into her own hands and gave her servant Hagar to Abraham so that she would have a child for them. Her servant conceived and then felt contempt for Sarah who, with her husband's permission, chose to deal harshly with her servant, even though she had created the situation (again, lots of sin and brokenness). Hagar gave birth to Ishmael. Later in the story, God tells Abraham that he will be the father of nations, and although he thinks God will use Ishmael, God had a different plan. Sarah, in her old age (91), became pregnant, and had a child named Isaac with whom God established His covenant of nations.

As you can see, God uses broken people to carry out His will. I have been blessed by their stories of failure and success and encouraged by God's hand through it all. He puts us in particular circumstances in order that we would learn the richness of *depending on Him* instead of on ourselves. Through our trials and successes, He is the one who receives the glory, because He is the one doing the good work in us. Praise God!

We have also been learning during our study, through the women above, as well as the story of the Israelites, that God brings us to a turning point where we need to decide to turn away, take a step of faith, have that tough conversation, or do whatever it takes. From there, we need to *endure the wilderness faithfully.* Another story from the old testament brought this to light so clearly. In Genesis 22, Abraham was asked by God to sacrifice His own son (yes, the one who was to be father of many nations, with whom God had established His covenant). He traveled with his son, Isaac, for *three* days through the desert to get to the mount where he was to commit the sacrifice. Now, three days doesn't seem that long–especially when you're on vacation and time just flies by, but three days while contemplating, praying, and dreading a moment like having to sacrifice your son? I'm sure that time didn't "fly by" for Abraham.

Nevertheless, *he wasn't fearful*, because he knew that God would provide, as long as he obeyed.

If you've never read or heard the story, that is *exactly* what happened! Abraham had brought Isaac up the mountain and even had him bound, ready to become an obedient sacrifice, when God sent a ram to be offered in the place of Isaac. Praise God for His provision and Abraham's faithfulness, because out of that situation, not only was Isaac saved, but an entire nation was able to prosper. We don't always understand why God asks us to do certain things, or wait for days or years, or even deliver plagues on Egypt (there's Moses again), but we don't need to understand His reasoning. All we need to do is obey, *dwell in His presence,* and trust that He has it all under control.

Our pastor's summer series is about drawing close to God. He has preached on Moses, Hannah, and Sarah. Clearly, God is trying to tell me something here! I am not the first person to suffer in this way (duh!), and He sees the suffering of His children. He has seen it from the very beginning. He knows His children and, "we know that in all things, God works for the good of those who love Him, who have been called according to His purpose (Romans 8:28, NIV)." I am so thankful that Chris and I are not in control of this situation. Rather than us trying to say the perfect thing in our profile or answer just the right way on our questionnaire, we can rest confidently in the fact that we serve a big God who knows our hearts and knows what will happen. He is working all things for good.

So in this time of waiting, we continue to learn more about our savior. Who He is and who He created us to be. I am thankful that we can go to Him with our heart's desires and that He hears our prayers. We are preparing our hearts and our home for our little one and are *celebrating in anticipation* of the good work that God will do!

Those were some raw, unfiltered moments from our adoption journey. At the writing of this chapter, that last blog post was seventeen months ago, and we are still waiting. Although we trust that God's timing is perfect and much better than our own, the waiting is hard. The nursery is ready, but empty. Our arms are ready, but empty. We have been aiming for contentment and are definitely grateful for the blessings we have, but are acutely aware of the one that we don't have yet.

The year 2020 has been filled with unknowns, trials, difficulties, and lots of joy hidden between all of those tough moments. Sometimes you just had to look closely. Covid-19 has truly affected every part of our lives, including the adoption. The agency has seen less mothers come through their doors as all of the counseling and pre-labor services have gone virtual. I cannot imagine how difficult it is to try to make a life-altering decision like creating an adoption plan for your baby, let alone having to do it over Zoom!

We had a slight scare early in 2021. Chris was having body aches for about a week. He tested positive for Covid on day seven of symptoms. As per usual when one of us is sick, we had already been sleeping in separate beds. I was still feeling great, but decided to get tested to alleviate some anxiety for family members.

I tested positive.

Still without symptoms, we thought it could be a false positive. Either way, we wanted to be safe, so we both started a strict vitamin regiment, prayed, and enlisted our prayer warriors as well. The weather was nice, so we were able to be outside, which was the only time we were in each other's presence. FaceTime was a life saver, but also, prayer. Each morning that I awoke symptomless, I rejoiced and thanked God. Now, whether it really was Covid, or just my terrible seasonal allergies, I did have several days where I wasn't able to taste or smell much. Besides that, I did not get sick at all, which we are so thankful for! Surprisingly, doctors were no help—even my specialists. Chris recovered after thirteen days of fairly mild symptoms, and I made it out of quarantine feeling fine. Really, it was the best situation for me, as I now have the antibodies that will help my body protect itself in the future, and I didn't have to worry about getting sick.

As we wait, we continue to pray for those who have dreadfully been affected by the woes of this pandemic. Chris and I have finished the nursery, acquired some clothes and accessories from family and friends, and further discussed what life will look like with a little one. We have both been working from home for the past eleven months and are enjoying each other's company. I have also had more time to work on this book and am so thankful and overwhelmed as I sit here at my kitchen table and type these last few words.

I've been asked a few times how I would end my book since I have so much life left to live, and this is my answer:

Research is ongoing, searching for a cure for many diseases.
Although we can't put our hope in modern medicine, it
is amazing and has radically changed many lives for the
better. I am thankful for those who devote their lives to
the betterment of others'. As such, advocacy and awareness
are critical as we all work together to find answers.

Life is full of opportunities, open doors, and joyful moments.
It can also bring fear, anxiety, and uncertainty. Choose
wisely which of these you will dwell on and embrace.

The only constant is God. He is good, He is faithful, He never
leaves us, and He knows our hearts and His plan for our lives.
As long as we are trusting that, we have nothing to fear.

This hope
IS A STRONG
&
TRUSTWORTHY
anchor for our
SOULS
It leads us through
the curtain
→ into →
God's inner sanctuary

Hebrews 6:19
NLT

EPILOGUE

Since the conference in 2017, I have had a few other unexplainable symptoms pop up. A month after the conference, my abdomen started swelling. It was a few pounds at first, but over the course of three months, I had gained about fifteen pounds and was fluctuating an average of four or five pounds a day. My clothes barely fit, and at times, my stomach was distended up to three inches! I was having some digestion and intestinal issues, which I assumed were directly impacted by the swelling. We visited Dr. Lee and he ran some tests to ensure that my kidney function was still normal. Thankfully, it was, but that offered no direction for treatment. By Thanksgiving, the swelling was hardly noticeable, so I didn't continue to ask the doctors about it.

The following summer the right side of my face started feeling numb. It started around my jawline for a few days, but continued into my cheek and eventually there was tingling on the entire right side. My internist suggested that I see my neurologist because it might be trigeminal neuralgia. From my own internet sleuthing, it didn't seem like my symptoms were as severe nor as painful as the ones caused by that condition, but Chris and I determined we should see him anyway.

We drove the quick hour to the hospital, got my head CT, and then waited for two hours in the doctor's office. The nurse's only explanation for the delay was that doctor Zwag was in surgery and she wasn't sure when he would appear. Waiting in doctor's offices is one of my least favorite pastimes, but it seems to be an unavoidable evil.

Doctor Zwag came in swiftly and apologized for the delay. To his credit, he was completely present with us and had no lingering headspace from surgery. It's rather amazing that doctors can transition this quickly. Especially from doing brain surgery to being face to face with a patient discussing dramatic life changes. His news was easily delivered because it was fairly good news. There was no physical evidence of any nerve damage or anything else that could be causing the numbness. He asked if there was pain with the numbness, to which I was able to answer that it had only been occasional. Although it was sharp and sometimes breath-taking, it lasted no more than a few seconds. So, we heard the words "we're just not sure," again and were told to update him if anything changed. He also offered up the 33% prognosis, letting me know that it would either get better, get worse, or stay the same. You don't really need medical school for that one, but what was he supposed to say?

My face is still numb and definitely worsens with any other swelling in my body or any sickness, but I hardly notice it anymore. I think that is mostly because I know it's nothing that needs significant surgery or intervention. It could've gotten worse, and it didn't; so for that, I am praising God!

The weird abdominal swelling has returned over the last year, along with the GI issues. My specialist and internist didn't have much to say about it. I was referred to a gastrointestinal doctor who performed an upper endoscopy that didn't yield any significant results. Similar to the first time, the swelling has caused discomfort, sometimes pain, and an increase in pant size. We don't yet know if it's related to GLA, but if it's not, it's another weird symptom of something else. So, we continue on the journey of hopeful discovery and maintaining a good quality of life.

That's just part of the reality of living with a rare disease.

WORKS CONSULTED

Fritz, Annie L. "10 Essential Facts About Rare Disease." *Everyday Health,* 12 February 2020, https://www.everydayhealth.com/news/10-essential-facts-about-rare-diseases/.

Krans, Brian and Adcox, Mariah. "What is a PET scan?" *Healthline,* 29 June 2020, https://www.healthline.com/health/pet-scan#followupand-results.

Lymphangiomatosis and Gorham's Disease Alliance. "About the Alliance." Lymphangiomatosis & Gorham's Disease Alliance: Patient Driven Solutions for Complex Lymphatic Anomalies, https://www.lgdalliance.org/about-the-alliance-2/. Accessed 26 September 2018.

National Organization for Rare Disorders. "Rare Disease Database." *NORD,* https://rarediseases.org/for-patients-and-families/information-resources/rare-disease-information/. Accessed 18 June 2019.

Office of Neuroscience Communications and Engagement. "Chiari Malformation Fact Sheet." *National Institute of Neurological Disorders and Stroke,* https://www.ninds.nih.gov/chiari-malformation-fact-sheet#8. Accessed 14 March 2019.

Made in United States
Orlando, FL
18 May 2023